THEY THINK YOU'RE STUPID

Stroud & Hall Publishers
P.O. Box 27210
Macon, Ga 31221
www.stroudhall.com

The paper used in this publication meets the minimum requirements
of American National Standard for Information Sciences—
Permanence of Paper for Printed Library Materials.
ANSI Z39.48–1984. (alk. paper)

Library of Congress Cataloging-in-Publication Data

Cain, Herman.
They think you're stupid : why Democrats lost your vote and what Republicans must do to keep it
by Herman Cain.

p. cm.

ISBN 0-9745376-0-8
(hardback : alk. paper)
1. Political parties—United States.
2. Politics, Practical—United States.
3. Political participation—United States.
4. United States–Politics and government.
5. Conservatism—United States.
I. Title: They think you're stupid.
II. Title.

JK2265.C25 2005   324'.0973--dc22

2005003156hhh

THEY THINK YOU'RE STUPID

Why Democrats Lost Your Vote and
What Republicans Must Do to Keep It

Dedication To

My mother, Lenora Davis Cain
(80 years young in 2005)

Table of Contents

Acknowledgements

Thank You!

To God, who continues to bless me beyond my wildest dreams.

To my family and wife, Gloria, for all their love, support, joy and even laughter, especially when I get too sleepy and make no sense at all.

MATT CARROTHERS for his invaluable collaboration, research skills and dedication to the timely completion of this project.

Ericka Pertierra, Karleen Mahn and Joel Ricks for their brutally honest feedback, even if I did not like it.

Mary and Eric Tanenblatt for making their "hideaways" available for my writing retreats.

All of the staff, financial donors, and faithful volunteers who worked on the Cain for U.S Senate Campaign of 2004.

All of the voters in Georgia who voted for me and encouraged me to keep my voice and message heard. I hear you and stay tuned.

Randy Evans for suggesting that I write this book.

Stroud and Hall Publishers for their professionalism and willingness to truly be a partner in this project.

Senator Zell Miller for his inspiration as a leader, a true statesman, and an unwavering speaker of the truth.

To everyone who has prayed for me and my family. Thank you.

—Herman Cain

Herman Cain writes "they don't get it." I think he should add to that "and they're gonna get it." Herman Cain writes that politicians are clueless about the average Joe, and folks are getting tired of it. Politicians who don't care for their constituents are going to be tossed out on their ears, as well they should be.

Today's political arena needs leaders who know people, real people. Not the cookie cutter demographic techno-speak spat out by some pollster. Real people have real problems and need real solutions. But you can't lead toward the solution that the promise of America holds out if you don't know or care about the voters. What keeps them up late at night? What are their struggles? What gets them up early? What are their dreams?

Herman Cain knows and has proven that the voting public is neither stupid, nor are they giving up. When he ran in the Republican primary for the U.S. Senate in Georgia, the political "experts" wrote Cain off as a novelty. For all the media's pride over its progressiveness, they don't know what to think of a black and conservative Republican other than "he's a novelty." How's that for respect? Herman Cain breathed a breath of fresh and honest air in a politics-as-usual race. He brought a platform based on true respect for the taxpayer, solutions based on the same kind of common sense that have made him a self-made business success story.

Herman Cain also did something few politicians can duplicate. He brought in new voters. The politician who can bring new voters to the booth is reflecting the light of the American Dream itself. Herman Cain motivated college students with his message of responsibility and opportunity. Herman Cain attracted both Democrats and Republicans who were eager for a fresh start and some common sense.

Cain writes that even though he didn't win the nomination, he didn't lose either. His goal was to serve the people of Georgia. He did more than that by ensuring the truly important issues were addressed during the campaign and not simply danced around with sound bites. It takes a steady man who is sure of himself not to be distracted by the needs of his own ego. You can know there's something good about a man whose ultimate goal is to help others by representing them well.

All party leaders would do well to listen to him. Cain is onto something important for our future. The kind of democracy we have enjoyed for more than two hundred years won't survive voter apathy. When the voters' trust is lost, so is their support. To their own demise, many politicians play the politics-as-usual game and continue to think of voters as mindless and willing to follow anyone because of a few well-placed jabs and sound bites. Candidates from either party who are more concerned with how the party fares will find themselves with plenty of free time on their hands. Cain is the kind of man who is willing even to alienate himself from his own political party to do what's right. He ran for the U.S. Senate here in Georgia without the party bosses' blessing. He ran well. And it took a very good man to defeat him. I know something of what it means to be ostracized by party leaders, even from the party I've supported my entire political career. I also know something of the peace of mind that comes from doing the right thing and taking the right stand and holding the right ground. Doing the right thing can make a politician lonely at the Capitol, but satisfied in spirit. Herman Cain and his wise and proven leadership are a force to be reckoned with by politicians and a lifeline to the voter who wants common sense leadership but feels like an outsider in both parties.

Cain's *New Voice* and its aim to educate and inspire the disenfranchised or "homeless" voter gives me hope. I'm on his side because I'm on the side of anyone who cares for this country with honesty, good horse sense, and strong character. Herman Cain is that kind of leader.

Zell Miller
Former U.S. Senator and Governor of Georgia

Preface

This book is intended to be a wake-up call to both the Democratic Party and the Republican Party. If they both stay asleep at the wheel, then this book can become a mobilizing force for the millions of voters who feel politically homeless. Many people have a party affiliation as a practical matter, but more and more people are finding it harder to feel a deep sense of loyalty to either party. Party insiders will disagree, and therein lies the problem. They don't see that there is a problem. They see the next election and the next campaign. Party outsiders want to see more results.

When I ran as a conservative Black Republican in the 2004 election for the U.S. Senate in Georgia, the party faithful considered me as an outsider because I had not asked permission from the Republican Party leaders in Georgia, nor had I ever sought any elective office before. A longtime Republican insider advised me that my chances of winning were very slim. He was only half right. They were slim, but not *very* slim. I won an impressive second place in the Republican primary. It is this experience that has made me aware of the rising tide of the politically homeless.

I have no illusions that many Democratic Party insiders will read this book; they are nearing political bankruptcy and cannot see it coming. The title for this book, *They Think You're Stupid*, evolved as I wrote. I have seen how many Democratic candidates distort, ignore, and even change the facts to try to get elected.

Although Republicans are not innocent in this regard, their political capital is on the rise, and they have not backed themselves into an ideological corner that cannot be dramatically improved. In fact, my own party has a unique opportunity to dominate the political landscape for decades if they do a better job of reaching out to the party outsiders with results, rather than waiting for outsiders to reach in. It is my hope for this nation that the Republican Party will embrace some of the ideas that I present in this book in order to achieve sustained political dominance.

For the politically homeless, the political outsiders, or the political dropouts, I hope this book gives you a renewed sense of hope that we do not have to settle for politics as usual and results as usual.

—*Herman Cain*

My name is Herman Cain, and I used to be stupid. This is because I did not know the history of the Democratic Party, nor did I know the history of the Republican Party. Like millions of voters, I used to make my voting decisions based on news sound bites, political labels, distortions, misinformation, and sometimes no information at all. Although I have been voting Republican in federal elections since 1980, and I even ran for elected office as a Republican in 2004, I often felt *politically homeless* on the big issues. I am now a graduate of "Stupid Anonymous" and want to share my awakening with others.

I was never the smartest kid in class when I was growing up, but I was usually among the fastest learners. This has served me well in my business career, which many people would consider successful by most measures. For this reason, I have the nerve to express my views on the world of politics after only one run for elective office (U.S. Senate Republican 2004 Georgia primary). I finished second, but it was an impressive second. More importantly, I learned some valuable lessons swimming in the pool of politics while wearing the goggles of the business world.

The Democratic Party is losing voters in droves, but those same voters are not joining the Republican Party in like droves. Democrats can't keep voters because their usual rhetoric has been exposed as empty. Republicans can't get these voters because their rhetoric doesn't resonate with many of them. These voters may be voting for Republicans, but they are not as truly Republican as those inside the party would like to believe.

The elections of 2004 illustrate that the Democratic Party is between a rock and a hard place. One prominent Democratic governor believes the massive Democratic losses at the state and federal levels and the presidency were due to the party's failure to use the right words to communicate with the public. She has not yet realized that maybe the problem is the lack of content in the message.

Political pundits, consultants, and analysts have tried to explain the 2004 election results by way of a swing group of voters. They are in denial that when more than one hundred million people vote, a majority of them are smart enough to think for themselves and not as a group.

The Republican Party is also between a rock and a hard place. They won the presidency and control of both houses of Congress in 2004. The "rock" is the responsibility to lead and fix the big issues, which have gone unfixed for decades. The "hard place" is the prospect of being back in the minority in a few years if they choose to maintain the status quo in Washington, D.C. Voters are hungry for common sense, a sense of urgency, and real leadership.

The Republican and Democratic parties have emerged as a two-"plantation" system in these early years of the twenty-first century. Both parties want voters to stay or join because of tradition or their intraparty rules, instead of offering clear and compelling ideological positions. They are moving farther and farther apart, leaving an increasing number of voters with a sense of being politically homeless. This group includes Democrats, Republicans, Independents, and registered non-voters who are put off by the scare tactics, deception, distortions, and lack of real new solutions to the biggest problems.

The politically homeless are a large and growing percentage of the electorate, and they want to be heard. More importantly, they want to make things happen differently and at a faster pace in Washington, D.C. The politically homeless are a rising tide of *new voices* who feel more and more disconnected to their traditional party affiliations and are uninspired by both Republicans and Democrats.

These new voices come from all races, ages, backgrounds, and political affiliations. They have in common a desire to be inspired again by the promise of our great nation. New voices want political parties, political candidates, and elected officials to stop using the same decades-old political rhetoric and spin tactics against each other and on the public. They want solutions, not excuses. They want their president and their representatives in the U.S. House and Senate to place the interest of the people before the interest of the party. These new voices want leaders they can believe and believe in.

In the early history of this nation, the political parties used to command party loyalty because of clear ideological positions. The issues were not nearly as numerous as they are today and not even close in complexity. Today the parties try to demand party loyalty based on traditional reasons, and when someone strays from the plantation they are criticized, minimized, labeled, and then declared an outcast by the party faithful. Just ask former congressman J. C. Watts, who like me left the Democratic plantation long ago in favor of the Republican Party's commitment to conservative beliefs. Or ask Senator Zell Miller, whose book *A National Party No More: The Conscience of a Conservative Democrat* records his realization that the Democratic Party had long ago left him, rather than the opposite.

This book makes the case for why voters are not as dumb as Democrats think, and why voters are smarter than Republicans think. Too many people inside the major political parties have forgotten that we are all in the same boat now. Terrorists want to kill all of us. The current tax code and Social Security structure will bankrupt all of us. The Medicare mess is driving the costs of health care up and its quality down for all of us. We are all citizens of the United States of America first. These big, bodacious, unsolved problems are the enemies of us all. We are all in the same floundering boat.

This book will also illustrate the factors responsible for the large and growing base of new voices. It will examine why conservative White Democrats and young African-Americans are leaving the Democratic plantation. I will also discuss why these voters do not immediately feel comfortable with the Republican Party and why Republicans experience difficulty inspiring many supporters in their traditional voter base. More importantly, this book will identify how this group of new voices can be informed and inspired to become a deciding force on major issues and solutions.

I want to be clear that in this assessment of the parties, I am *not* advocating the creation of a third political party for those who feel politically homeless. Rather, my purpose is to force the existing parties and Congress to focus more on the history-changing big issues and their solutions and to use clear and compelling facts to engage the public. The party that does not embrace such a strategy is headed for extinction. Why? Because the public is waking up to "say-anything-to-get-elected" politics. They think we're stupid, but we're not.

I also want to inspire voters to become more informed. We must all become more engaged in the critical issues our nation faces. If the new voices do not get more involved in the political process between elections, their elected and party officials have little incentive to change the nature of political campaigns or the status quo in Washington, D.C.

Life, liberty, and the pursuit of happiness are ideals we must protect. We must preserve these ideals with a more informed and inspired public. If we do not, we will not leave our grandchildren a mess—we will leave them a disaster.

I believe in the "new nation" as conceived by our Founding Fathers. And I believe we can create a new day in the history of that new nation.

Chapter One

They Just Don't Get It

The Political Parties Alienate Voters

Both the Democrats and the Republicans have talked a long time about being inclusive and having a "big tent." They think their tents are getting bigger, but they are not. Their tents are simply getting wider and becoming filled with more constituents at opposite ends of many issues—issues that will not create increased economic opportunity for Leroy and Bessie Public and their family. Every issue is the most important issue to someone, but some issues are most important to everyone:

> Winning the war on terror.
> Winning the war on our moral foundation.
> Winning the war on our economic infrastructure.

Bitter disputes and partisan gridlock arise over what is considered winning and what is considered important. Our

Founding Fathers believed in country first, self-interests second, and political parties a distant third. Unfortunately, too many politicians today have these priorities reversed. Many current political leaders place the interests of their political party first, to the detriment of the best interests of the country. Three hundred million people will never agree 100 percent on everything, but we can agree on a few big things with the right priorities. That's when we all win.

The Republicans and the Democrats suffer from a deficiency of effective leadership—not all of their leaders, but most of their leaders. Leadership requires removing barriers to self-motivation, working on the right problems, and inspiring people to feel connected to the right results. The most successful businesses understand this. The political parties do not. This was the most glaring observation I made as a result of actually running for the U.S. Senate with a personal history of thirty-five years as a businessman.

As the parties' tents get wider, more barriers are created that drive people out or keep them away. The candidates who get elected to Congress quickly lose focus and spend a lot of time working on the wrong problems. Worse, they are forced into trying to fix some of the wrong solutions to the wrong problems of the past. The best example is the Social Security system. It has been broken for decades, and we are still not anywhere close to fixing it. One of my opponents, a congressman, said, "Congress does not act until there's a crisis." I wonder what the definition of a crisis is in Congress when we are talking about the Social Security system. Someone is in gross denial.

Both political parties routinely create barriers to voter self-motivation by working on the wrong problems. Working on the wrong problems makes it impossible to inspire voters. The most recent example is the prescription drug bill. Even though some in Congress will tout how much this legislation helped Grandma save on prescription drugs, Leroy and Bessie intuitively know that $544 billion spent on a one-size-fits-all program will eventually backfire. The right solution in this case would have been to establish an assistance program for the 20 percent of seniors who had no prescription drug coverage. According to the Heritage Foundation, with the right cost containment incentives this solution would have cost a little more than one hundred billion dollars.

The Republicans try to inspire voters on principle. The principle that workers should keep more of their hard-earned money is a good example. This is achieved through tax cuts on income and investments, which stimulate the economy, which pays for existing jobs and new jobs, and which makes it possible for businesses to pay workers even more money. This principle is called *elementary economics*. Unfortunately, elementary economics gets lost in the clutter of strong emotional rhetoric and distortions. As a result, many people disregard the principle of elementary economics when deciding for whom to cast their vote.

The usual Democrat strategy of inspiring voters is to invoke class warfare, which is often packaged with race baiting, victimization, and fear. We have heard hundreds of times the rhetoric "It is just a tax cut for the rich," or the promise by a candidate to somehow "Take from the rich and give it to those who need it." The Democrats are certainly not going to tell people, "You should keep less of your hard-earned money. We want the government to take more of your money, which is achieved through tax increases, which stifles the economy, which reduces jobs, and which causes businesses to pay fewer people even less money, or even cause businesses to go out of business."

In the early history of this nation, an honest candidate could inspire people with an honest message from a town square, the back of a train, or a real town hall meeting. Today, principle and honesty can get lost in the around-the-clock sound bites produced in the fast-paced media and political advertising world. As a result, more and more people are unable or do not take the time to connect the dots to find the truth and make an informed voting decision. Professional politicians know this and exploit it to their advantage.

Political leaders have many opportunities to *inspire* people to vote. People want to be informed and inspired. They want to connect to issues intellectually and emotionally. Voters want to know how an issue affects them, their families, and the nation. If voters do not see how an issue personally affects them and their families, they will not feel connected to the message or the messenger.

The debate surrounding repeal of the federal estate tax provides a great example. Until recently, most African-Americans felt no connection to this debate because they did not have any estates to pass on to their heirs. My great-grandparents were sharecroppers who owned no land, no homes, and no businesses. They had no sellable assets other than their own sweat equity. When my maternal great-grandfather died at the age of ninety-four, the estate he left his family was his good name and his reputation. Three generations later, my brother and I were part of the first generation of college graduates in our family and, in my case, a successful restaurant business owner. Many other African-American families share a similar story. A large and growing percentage of African-Americans have achieved some financial success, which has produced a personal connection to arguments for eliminating the estate tax.

The current estate tax does not merely "tax the rich" as the Democratic Party has argued for years. It causes farmers to have to sell the farm to try to save the farm and unfairly diminishes the ability to pass first-generation success on to the next generation in a family. A lifetime of hard work and risk-taking should not go to the government, but to one's family.

Another example is restructuring Social Security versus putting another band-aid on the system. When I addressed a group of African-American ministers in Fitzgerald, Georgia, I stated, "The Social Security structure is bad for everybody, but it is worse for Black people." I explained that because of the average life expectancy for Black men—sixty-eight years, versus seventy-five years for Whites—Blacks can expect on average only a few years of low benefits from the Social Security system.

The current Social Security structure is broken and has been for decades, and it is headed for certain bankruptcy. Social Security must be totally restructured. It does not make sense to pay into a broken structure for more than forty years only to receive minimal benefits for four or five years. For too long, though, Blacks and millions of others have been told that Republicans want to rob their Social Security benefits and give the money to the rich in the form of tax cuts. Of course, this deceptive rhetoric could not be farther from the truth.

One of the ministers stood up and challenged the group to spread this information throughout their communities. Others nodded in agreement. Another minister asked why they had not heard these statistics before. I responded that "they" did not want them to know these facts. The ministers had now made an intellectual and emotional connection to the issue of restructuring Social Security.

The fact that more than half of all registered voters in the United States do not exercise their right to vote shows that a higher than acceptable percentage of the electorate is uninformed and uninspired about the issues and government. An uninformed electorate is particularly susceptible to fear-based rhetoric, and they tend to believe negative messages. *Information counteracts fear-based rhetoric, and compelling facts counteract negative messages.*

The Politics of Politics

The professional politicians from both political parties in Congress spend too much time engaging in the "politics of politics" instead of honestly representing their constituents and working to enact policies that will protect the economic infrastructure for our grandchildren. The politics of politics are activities that tend to do more to improve a politician's campaign war chest and his or her political career than actually to find solutions to the biggest issues that confront us.

One example of politicians spending time on the politics of politics is when a senator or representative promises his or her vote on a piece of legislation in return for the guarantee of a big (pork barrel) appropriation for his or her district. Other examples abound. Instead of showing leadership in Congress by working on enacting aggressive policy solutions, many representatives tell their constituents and the media, "I co-sponsored legislation" or "I introduced legislation" that addresses a particular issue. The real question is, "How hard did you work to get the legislation passed?"

Other members like to remove themselves symbolically from Congress when addressing their constituents or the media. They will defend their inaction by saying, "Congress is always in gridlock" or "There are people up there who just want to block everything. I'm fighting for you, but it is tough to take on 534 others who also want bills passed."

These excuses are laughable given that every year, members of Congress seem to have no problem working with each other when it comes time to send billions of our tax dollars back to their districts for projects that should be funded at the state and local levels. Every minute and every day members of Congress spend engaged in the politics of politics is an opportunity lost to work on the real issues that confront us, such as replacing the federal tax code and restructuring the Social Security system. Time spent on the politics of politics allows Congress to avoid tackling the big, often controversial issues, thereby increasing their chances for reelection.

The politics of politics differ greatly from the politics of business. In business, your performance is evaluated every day, every fiscal quarter, and every year. Businessmen place results ahead of politics. Politicians place politics ahead of results.

Business executives and small business owners are in constant competition for consumers' dollars and must answer to their constituents—consumers—or they will soon be out of business. With a few exceptions, most businesses must meet their consumers' demands, provide the highest levels of customer service, and provide a high-quality product.

Members of Congress need to accept that voters are not turned off by the ideas of replacing the tax code, restructuring Social Security, and protecting our moral foundations. They are turned off to the legislative process by politicians who are afraid to lead on these big issues. Voters want issue leadership, not squeamish politicians who would rather trade votes for pork and make constant excuses.

As a chief executive officer (CEO) or small business owner, you may be tempted to hire someone you have known, is a friend, or looks like you. But you also understand that you must hire and promote the most qualified people, regardless of how they look or your familiarity with them, to meet your business goals and survive. Voters need to consider themselves responsible CEOs of this country and take ownership in their government every election day. Voters have the responsibility to monitor the activities of their elected leaders and ensure that only those politicians who have demonstrated aggressive issue leadership are awarded the privilege to represent their state or districts for another term. Voters can end the politics of politics that diminish our chances to tackle the big issues, but only if they become more responsible owners of their government and the political process.

Lessons of 1994

The "Republican Revolution" of 1994 gave Republicans a fifty-two-seat pickup in the U.S. House of Representatives and made the Democrats the House minority party for the first time in forty years. Democrats could not accept the reality of defeat at that time, and they struggle with being the minority party to this day.

In 1994, I spent a lot of time in Washington, D.C. when I served as chairman of the National Restaurant Association. A Georgia Democratic congressman and fellow Morehouse College alumni and friend called me shortly after the Republican takeover. We talked and agreed to meet for lunch. A few days later we went to one of his favorite lunch spots—a Washington, D.C. church that serves great Southern cooking. On the way to lunch, I asked the congressman how he and his party were dealing with their new status as minority in the U.S. House. He sort of dropped his head for a second and said, "We don't have control anymore. We don't have control anymore." Several times during lunch he repeated, "We don't have control anymore."

I said to him, "You are in Washington to represent all the constituents in your district, both Republicans and Democrats. You and your party are not in control anymore, but do you really think the Republicans are going to turn out to be some sort of devils just because they are now in control after forty years of Democratic control?"

Again, he repeated, "We're not in control anymore."

It was clear that the congressman and the members of his party did not know how to think, how to act, or how to compromise from a position that did not control Congress. They had never had to compromise with the majority, because for most of them they had always been that majority. In the last ten years as the minority party, the apparent strategy of the Democrats has been to obstruct, attack, and discredit any idea or proposal that is considered a Republican idea.

I asked a California congressman once why he could not support the idea of totally restructuring Social Security since the current system is clearly broken. He responded, "We can't do anything that might make President Bush and the Republicans look good." When did "for the good of the political party to regain control" overtake "for the good of the country and the people"? This Democratic strategy has driven many voters into the politically homeless zone.

In sharp contrast to the Democrats' expectations of "Republican devils" in control of Congress in 1994, the Republicans produced a positive, forward-thinking people's agenda called the Contract with America. Former Georgia congressman and Speaker of the House Newt Gingrich and his colleagues wrote the Contract with America prior to the 1994 elections. They voted on all ten of the contract's policy issues within the first one hundred days of the next legislative session and succeeded in passing nine. The contract was a clear policy agenda that focused on restoring in the U.S. House accountability to the public while reducing the size and influence of federal government. It focused on budget and spending restraint, personal responsibility, and economic prosperity for individuals and businesses.

Perhaps the most important feature of the Contract with America was that it connected its policy initiatives to common sense benefits that Leroy and Bessie Public could understand. Speaker Gingrich was a leader who successfully communicated to the public that the Republicans were not going to squander their new majority status.

In the Contract with America, Republicans offered a focused policy agenda and escalated American political discourse about the proper influence of government. The Contract with America inspired millions of Americans to believe that significant policy changes were possible.

Democrats, however, relentlessly attacked Gingrich and the Republicans over the contract. The popularity of the contract, the swiftness with which its policies passed through the House, and Gingrich's leadership forced Democrats to go into an aggressive attack mode, where they remain to this day.

It can be argued that the Democrats' tactics produced some degree of success, as Speaker Gingrich was forced out of

Congress by 1998. That same year, the Republican Party, which expected to gain House seats, showed the poorest results in thirty-four years of any party not in control of the White House. Gingrich resigned from the Speakership and from his House seat in November 1998. Republicans retained control of the House and do to this day. But the departure of Gingrich left a leadership void in the Republican-controlled Congress that to a large extent has not been replaced.

I believe the Republican Revolution stalled for two reasons. First, during Newt Gingrich's tenure as Speaker of the House, not enough other Republican members felt a sense of ownership in the Contract with America. My thirty-five years of experience in the business world taught me that owners run things better than managers. Managers who share an ownership attitude in an operation run things much better than managers who feel they are just employees. When people feel a sense of ownership, they are much more motivated to achieve the desired results.

Since Bill Clinton, a Democrat, was president during most of the 1990s, Gingrich, as the highest-ranking elected Republican, was in many respects the face of the Republican Party nationally. It was easy for the political layperson to view the contract as "Newt's contract" instead of an agenda for the entire House Republican membership. Gingrich's departure in 1998 from the U.S. House therefore symbolized the departure of a clear Republican policy agenda.

The second reason the Republican Revolution stalled is that the Republican congressional majority became divided behind Newt's leadership. The Republicans were not solidly united behind Gingrich and his agenda in 1994, and many remain ideologically divided to this day. I believe this is due to the politics of politics, to which many longtime members of Congress have grown accustomed.

Gingrich received criticism from fellow Republicans when he negotiated in 1995 with President Clinton a reopening of the federal government. In addition, not all current House and Senate Republicans share the conservative wing's zeal for aggressive policy change. Many openly approve of increased federal spending and have moderate positions on social issues. Some Republicans formed the Republican Main Street Partnership, a group of moderates devoted to a centrist approach to law making.

The primary effect of the ideological divide is that the current Republican congressional majority lacks the ability to design a new, focused policy agenda similar to the Contract with America. Leaders of any organization must always challenge its constituency to focus on a new vision to keep the people inspired. Republican leaders fail to understand that they must demonstrate bold leadership by setting an aggressive policy agenda, formulate a strategy to pass that agenda, and explain the benefits of their agenda to voters in a compelling way.

This is not to imply that there are no individual examples of members capable and willing to advance aggressive policy change. One example of an aggressive policy proposal is House Resolution (HR) 25, introduced by Georgia congressman John Linder and senators Saxby Chambliss and Zell Miller. Passage of HR 25 will replace the outdated mess that is the federal tax code with the national retail sales tax, also known as the FairTax. Linder and Chambliss are joined by more than fifty-two Republicans and one Democrat in co-sponsoring this aggressive legislation. The FairTax will remove the current onerous tax burden from the backs of U.S. citizens and businesses and cause the U.S. economy to skyrocket. Passage of the FairTax will dramatically benefit all citizens, especially the lowest wage earners. If this is the case, and I firmly and truly believe it is, why don't more members of Congress officially support the FairTax? The answer is that most of the members are waiting to be led, or to trade their vote for some "pork" to be sent back home.

Prior to entering the U.S. Senate race in Georgia, I consulted with former U.S. congressman J. C. Watts. I asked Congressman

Watts about the culture of Congress, what I could expect if I were elected, and the nature of leadership in the U.S. House and Senate.

"About 15 percent of the members are interested in aggressive policy change, in setting and leading an agenda, and in taking their policy agenda to the people," he explained.

Congressman Watts continued, "Then you have about 15 percent who lead some of the committees, try to protect their sandbox, send some pork back home and get reelected."

"Well, what about the other 70 percent?" I asked.

Congressman Watts replied, "The remaining 70 percent are just happy to be there!"

Many conservatives throughout the nation are frustrated that they see in today's Republican congressional membership—in both the House and Senate—too many legislators who are "just happy to be there." They yearn for Republican leaders like Ronald Reagan and Newt Gingrich who were capable and willing to formulate visions and focused, aggressive policy agendas. And they are discouraged by either the inability or unwillingness of current congressional leaders to fight back against Democrats who filibuster legislation and continually deceive the public. Leadership cannot be left solely to the president, because he is a little busy leading our troops and running the most complex democracy in the world.

Reagan and Gingrich understood the needs of their nation and the world. They knew the public wanted to change the failed liberal policies of the past. They were not afraid to lead. They also understood that successful leaders in any endeavor take people where they would not go by themselves.

Today's Republican leaders in the U.S. House and Senate must assume the responsibility of leadership that their status as majority party demands. If they do not, they will soon be stripped of the opportunity to lead and find themselves in the same position they were in just ten years ago—the minority.

We Won in 2004!

The 2004 Georgia Republican U.S. Senate primary received a lot of national attention, because it was assumed that the winner would be a virtual lock to succeed retiring senator Zell Miller. It also attracted attention across Georgia and the nation because a largely unknown businessman, who also happened to be a conservative, African-American Republican, was attracting voters and rising in the polls every week with a positive message of hope and change and a common sense agenda.

Many of the so-called political experts predicted that I would finish a distant third. After all, I was running against two seasoned political veterans who had spent most of their lives in political office and who had the name identification throughout Georgia to show for it. As is often the case in life, the experts were wrong. They underestimated the powerful combination of inspired hope and a common sense message of aggressively facing our nation's biggest issues. They had no idea that so many voters were hungry for a change in the status quo and were willing to work hard for a candidate in whom they believed.

The experts saw a conservative African-American Republican as a novelty who wouldn't be embraced by a mostly White voter base. More than 173,000 voters enthusiastically embraced this novelty and my message. I am thankful to the Georgians who saw in my candidacy a real solutions agenda and the possibility that we can change Washington, D.C.

On July 20, 2004, I achieved an impressive second-place finish in the three-way primary contest versus two sitting U.S. Representatives. The central theme of my campaign was that we *can* change the status quo mentality so entrenched in our capital city if we first believe change is possible and then mobilize the voters to make the change happen.

We did not win the nomination, but we did not lose either. We *won* on the battlefield of big issues by forcing my opponents to address replacing the federal income tax code, restructuring the Social Security system, and reducing government influence in the health care system. These issues are now at the forefront of state and national debate. You can't imagine how happy I was to hear President Bush, on the night of his acceptance speech at the Republican National Convention, call for a "simpler, fairer, pro-growth" tax system! Common sense would suggest that keeping the incomprehensible eight-million-word mess we call the federal tax code is not a viable option.

We *won* people to the polls like Charlie from Cobb County, who, before this race, had never registered to vote. Charlie is in his forties and had given up on government! Now he proudly carries his voter registration card, and he did vote. Then there was Miss Irene from Thomas County, who is in her eighties. She made time each week to help my campaign by talking to everyone in her town about my candidacy. Miss Irene and her friend Lillian would come to every campaign speech I gave within a hundred miles of where they lived. Each time, Miss Irene would not let me leave without putting a folded one hundred dollar bill in my hand as a campaign contribution. There was Whitney from Fulton County, a young woman who sought me out during a taping for a television program with tears in her eyes to tell me about her mother. Whitney's mother had recently passed away following a brave fight against breast cancer. One of her mother's final wishes was to vote for me because she was excited about my message of hope and change for the future.

We *won* thousands of college students who vigorously volunteered to help in the campaign, and we *won* hundreds of high school students who could not even vote yet. A tenth grade student, Jade, was asked why so many young people were supporting Herman Cain. She replied, "He gave us something to be excited about." Priceless.

We *won* thousands of white, lifelong conservative Democrats who told me it is time to turn the page on the racial divisions of the past, and we *won* scores of African-Americans who voted Republican for the first time in their lives. My eighty-year-old mother was at the front of that line.

We did not lose. We *won* thousands and thousands of new voters—*new voices*— looking for a political home.

New Voters

These new voters did not work hard every day to support me because I was a lifelong friend or a known celebrity. They supported me because they heard a new voice of common sense and renewed hope for substantive change. Stories like those just mentioned are a reminder that the countless hours of hard work and sacrifice by so many people were not in vain. We succeeded in spreading a message of economic freedom through aggressive solutions and inspired motivation to every corner of Georgia. The message resonated with people who had never before voted, who had never voted Republican, or who never would have considered voting for an African-American.

I believe this *new voter* phenomenon is occurring across the nation. Although the 2004 Georgia primary attracted just over 30 percent of registered voters, the general election this last presidential election year attracted a record number of voters to the polls, well in excess of the usual 50 percent turnout.

Conservative Democrats are leaving their party because it has adopted liberal positions radically different from the values of mainstream society. Any group convinced that it is a "victim" flocks to the Democratic Party looking for relief in the form of money from the federal treasury. Democrats run and get reelected to office with proclamations that the answers to this nation's problems are to throw more money at broken structures like Social Security, Medicare, and now health care. Senator Zell Miller documents the state of the national Democratic Party exceptionally well in his book *A National Party No More*.

Conservative Republicans are looking for other options. They feel taken for granted when their candidates move to the ideological center in election years and abandon traditional Republican ideology. For example, fiscal responsibility or spending the people's money responsibly has long been a pillar of the Republican Party. But in the last four years of a Republican controlled Congress, discretionary spending has increased in double-digit fashion every year. The cumulative increase in discretionary spending has been nearly 40 percent in four years.

Increasing numbers of newly registered voters, including young African-Americans, refuse to identify with either party and instead consider themselves Independents. Many young people have given up on government and choose not to participate at all. That's not a solution. It's another problem. The result of this phenomenon is a growing number of people who feel *politically homeless.* This does not mean they do not identify with one of the major political parties for practical reasons. It means more and more people are discouraged, disappointed, and disgusted with politics and politicians as usual.

The new voters in Georgia—displaced Democrats, rebellious Republicans, irate Independents, and registered non-voters sitting on the sidelines—supported my campaign because they sought a new, positive voice that championed common sense solutions to the big issues.

These *new voters* are part of the *new voices* being heard across this nation. They will also be heard in Washington, D.C., and not just on election day.

They Just Don't Get It

The Political Parties Alienate Voters

- Both the Democrats and the Republicans have talked a long time about being inclusive and having a "big tent." Their tents are not getting bigger. They are simply getting wider, with more constituents at opposite ends of many issues. As a result, both parties are alienating more and more voters.
- The Republicans and the Democrats suffer from a deficiency of effective leadership. Leadership requires removing barriers to self-motivation, working on the right problems, and inspiring people to feel connected to the right results. The most successful businesses understand this. The political parties do not.

The Politics of Politics

- The "politics of politics" differ greatly from the "politics of business." In business, your performance is evaluated every day, every fiscal quarter, and every year. Businessmen place results ahead of politics. Politicians place politics ahead of results.
- Voters can end the "politics of politics" that diminish our chances to tackle the big issues, but only if they become more responsible owners of their government and the political process.

Lessons of 1994

- The "Republican Revolution" of 1994 made the Democrats the House minority party for the first time in forty years. Democrats could not accept the reality of defeat at that time, and they still struggle with being the minority party. Republicans are struggling with being the majority party.

We Won in 2004!

- On July 20, 2004, I achieved an impressive second-place finish in the three-way U.S. Senate Republican primary in Georgia versus two sitting U.S. Representatives. We did not win the nomination, but we did not lose. We won thousands and thousands of new voters who heard common sense solutions to the big issues.

New Voters

- The new voter phenomenon is occurring across the nation. Newly registered voters, young African-Americans, unhappy Democrats, and unhappy Republicans are refusing to strongly identify with either party.
- The result of this phenomenon is a growing number of people who feel politically homeless. More and more people are discouraged, disappointed, and disgusted with politics and politicians as usual.

Chapter Two

Politically Homeless

The *politically homeless* are voters frustrated with their favorite political party or discouraged by what they see as politics-as-usual from their party leaders and elected officials. Some of the politically homeless choose to stay with their party out of a sense of principle or tradition, but they do not actively support the party's candidates. Others leave their party and support Independent or third party candidates. Unfortunately, some choose not to participate in the political process at all. Their disappointment and disgust with what they see and hear in the political arena causes them to give up on government, our elected officials, and the possibility of aggressive policy change. A key contributor to the problem of political homelessness is the confusion caused, often intentionally, by the seemingly never-ending barrage of labels, phrases, and made-for-television sound bites we hear every day from our elected officials.

Labels and Empty Rhetoric

My father walked off of his family's small Tennessee dirt farm in 1943 at the age of eighteen with literally just the clothes on his back. He had no money and no car, but he did have three invaluable possessions: his belief in God, his belief in himself and his abilities, and his belief in the promise of the United States of America. Dad believed that if he worked hard enough and smart enough, he could achieve his version of the American Dream. His dream was to provide a home and food for his family and give his children a better start in life than he had. He achieved all his dreams, but it was not easy. My father worked three jobs—as a chauffeur, a barber, and a janitor—to achieve his dreams and make sure we always had a roof over our heads, food on the table, and the opportunity for my brother and me to pursue a college education.

When Dad walked off of that dirt farm, he did not consider himself a Republican and he did not consider himself a Democrat. He considered himself someone working on his American Dream. When he was eighteen, he had never heard the terms *conservative* or *liberal, right wing* or *left wing.* The party label did not mean much to him because a party label was not going to help him achieve his dreams.

Today someone might say Dad was "blue collar," a member of the "working class," or maybe even the "middle class." The truth is, he never looked at himself as a member of someone else's description of his class, and he did not have much time to care about someone else's label. When all your time is spent providing for your family and working on making your American Dream a reality, you do not focus on your economic situation today—you focus on building the situation you desire for tomorrow.

Soon after I turned eighteen years old, I signed up with the Selective Service and registered to vote. My early political views were shaped by my dad's views. He told me, "Don't just look at the party. Look at the people, the issues, and look at a candidate's principles and character." His open-mindedness on political issues was influenced by the fact that for more than twenty-five years he worked for a prominent Atlanta CEO. Dad's boss spoke often about business principles, how to make money, how to save money, and how to build a business. This prominent CEO was a Republican. Their professional relationship helped open Dad's eyes to the realities of being a Republican, versus the rhetoric about Republicans told for decades to Black people by the predominant Democratic Party. Dad didn't fall for the rhetoric.

Dad's advice on politics and politicians has served me well. Though I considered myself a Democrat until my early thirties, I was focused on my dreams, my family, and my career and did not spend much time watching or discussing politics. Around that time, Ronald Reagan was elected president of the United States. I was beginning to make some money in the business world, and I thought the economic policies President Reagan talked about made the most sense for businesses and my family's future.

It was easy for me to support President Reagan and the Republicans because Dad taught me to look at the candidate's character and the reasons behind his positions on the issues, instead of just party labels and sound-bite rhetoric. President Reagan's policies simply made the most sense to me. I started voting Republican in the 1980s and have always been proud of that decision.

Though my positions on the political issues have wavered little throughout my life, I honestly did not realize I was a conservative until I began my campaign for U.S. Senate. I am pro-life on the issue of abortion. I fully support the Second Amendment right to bear arms. I am opposed to a government-imposed quota system on hiring practices. I believe we must replace the out-of-date federal tax code, and I believe Congress must severely cut back on its wasteful spending. But I did not know the term *conservative* defined my belief system. Prior to initial consultations with my campaign consultants when I ran for the U.S. Senate in Georgia, no one had ever packaged my political views into a single term.

Most people know what they believe in and their positions on the various political issues, but they do not characterize themselves according to others' pre-packaged definitions. People do not wake up each morning and say, "I am a Black conservative Republican! What a great day this will be!" Instead, they more likely wake up and think, "I have to get to work in one hour, work hard at my job, keep my job, provide for my family, and hope the government doesn't do too much today to screw up my opportunities."

The insistence by the parties, politicians, and pundits to tag everyone with a label adds to the problem of political homelessness. People do not ask to be labeled, and most people do not want to be placed within someone else's narrow confines and strict definitions of their political ideology. Like my dad, most people are not completely conservative or completely liberal in their personal political ideology. Most people just want to work hard on achieving their version of the American Dream and support political candidates who stand for *common sense solutions to the big issues.*

The meanings and connotations of many of the political labels and phrases we hear every day on the radio, on television, or use ourselves have become distorted to the point that serious, rational political discussion is often impossible. If you asked one hundred people what the words "Republican," "Democrat," "conservative," "moderate," "liberal," "rich," "poor," "working class," and "middle class" mean, you might receive one hundred different answers. Controversial issues such as affirmative action and tax cuts likewise elicit highly emotional responses. Political leaders and our elected officials toss around phrases like "tax cuts for the rich" and "government handout" with little regard for educating voters on the facts behind the issues.

Our political lexicon has been denigrated to such an extent that people interested in learning more about politics and the issues find it difficult to learn about either. We scold our children for name-calling; we should hold our political leaders responsible for the label-calling epidemic.

Unfortunately, perception in politics often becomes reality. A few years ago, I was traveling from Omaha to South Sioux City, Nebraska, to deliver a speech to the South Sioux City Chamber of Commerce. A college sophomore named Scotty accompanied me that day as part of a job shadow project at his school.

I asked Scotty, "Do you know what Republicans and Democrats are?"

He said, "Those are political parties."

"Very good," I said. "What does a Democrat stand for and what does a Republican stand for?"

Scotty replied, "A Democrat stands for the little people and a Republican stands for the rich guy."

That was not the first time I had heard that perception of the political parties from a young African-American. Just as perception differs from reality in people's thinking about the political parties, confusion also reigns in the highly politicized issue of affirmative action. So much confusion surrounds the affirmative action debate that a brief history of the issue is in order.

In March 1961, President John F. Kennedy issued Executive Order 10925, which established the President's Committee on Equal Employment Opportunity (PCEEO). The mission of the PCEEO was to end discrimination in employment by the federal government and its contractors. President Lyndon B. Johnson issued a similar directive in September 1965 (see text box on following page).

Though the language in President Johnson's executive order was similar to that of President Kennedy's, Johnson's order went on to abolish the PCEEO, transfer its responsibilities to the secretary of labor, and authorize the secretary of labor to "adopt

President Kennedy's *Executive Order 10925* required every federal government contract to include the provision that "The contractor will not discriminate against any employee or applicant for employment because of race, creed, color, or national origin. The contractor will take affirmative action, to ensure that applicants are employed, and that employees are treated during employment, without regard to their race, creed, color, or national origin."

President Johnson's *Executive Order 11246* stated that "It is the policy of the Government of the United States to provide equal opportunity in Federal employment for all qualified persons, to prohibit discrimination in employment because of race, creed, color, or national origin, and to promote the full realization of equal employment opportunity through a positive, continuing program in each executive department and agency. The policy of equal opportunity applies to every aspect of Federal employment policy and practice."

such rules and regulations and issue such orders as he deems necessary and appropriate to achieve the purposes thereof."

In December 1971, President Richard M. Nixon's Labor Department issued Revised Order No. 4, which required all federal contractors to develop "an acceptable affirmative action program," including "an analysis of areas within which the contractor is deficient in the utilization of minority groups and women, and further, goals and timetables to which the contractor's good faith efforts must be directed to correct the deficiencies."

In the decades that followed, government programs at the federal, state, and local levels mandated a variety of requirements specifying preference be given to minorities in employment and in awarding of certain contracts. In addition, some universities and local school systems, as well as fire, police, and other departments throughout the country, implemented their own policies that imposed racial quotas in acceptance and hiring procedures.

Presidents Johnson and Nixon each made slight changes to President Kennedy's original executive order, though none used the word "quota." Most of the confusion over the affirmative action mandates today is the product of disparities in the numerous state and federal court rulings on the constitutionality of giving preferences based on government-mandated criteria.

To many, affirmative action has come to mean preferential treatment for minorities and reverse discrimination for Whites. The term "affirmative action" has been demagogued by those opposed to the policy to mean quotas or mandates to hire or promote employees on factors other than merit. Due to the many and varied policies of government, educational, and private entities throughout the United States, as well as the many court rulings that have been made on these policies, "affirmative action" has become in practice a meaningless yet polarizing phrase.

Even newspaper and television reporters fall prey to the use of labels and their multiple meanings. Reporters asked me numerous times during my campaign for U.S. Senate, "Do you support or oppose affirmative action?" My response was always, "That depends on what you mean by the term 'affirmative action.' Do you mean a policy of mandated hiring quotas based on sex and ethnicity, or do you mean equal access and opportunities for all citizens?"

Some reporters thought I was trying to be defensive or trying to avoid the question. I was not, however, going to help perpetuate the use of this highly polarizing term. I may not be able to educate every reporter who asks a question, but I'm not going to say I'm for or against a label that has so many meanings to so many different groups. When I denounced quotas, I didn't offend all the Black people I know. Most people—Black, White,

Asian, whatever—are against quotas. At the same time, most people support removing barriers and equalizing opportunities, not outcomes.

Affirmative action stands with the economy as the most purposely confused and politicized issue in the modern political arena. When you ask an economist to define the economy or the current status of the economy, he or she will give you a much different answer than if you posed the same question to Leroy and Bessie Public. The economist will likely respond with a detailed account of current economic indicators, such as the Gross Domestic Product, unemployment rate, Consumer Confidence Index, corporate profit levels, and the status of the stock and bond markets.

Leroy and Bessie Public, however, will give you a definition that relates to their personal economic situation. If Leroy and Bessie are employed, able to pay all their bills, and can save a little money for the future, the current state of the economy is great! If they happen to be in a bad economic condition, though, and perhaps one of them has been laid off and the dollar is not stretching as far as it used to, then the economy is doing terribly.

The fact is, most people do not understand and are not aware of the myriad of metrics that provide us with the clearest possible perspective on the status of the economy. Most people tend to personalize the economic situation and feel that the status of the economy is a direct reflection on their current personal situation. Professional politicians know this, of course, and capitalize on voter misinformation and apathy with often confusing rhetoric.

That is why you often hear politicians discuss the economy in terms of jobs; jobs lost since their opponent took office and the unemployment rate are two favorites. "Jobs" is a label that appeals to people on a personal and emotional level. While the employment rate is in reality an outcome of a healthy economy, and not necessarily an indicator of economic growth in all sectors, Gross Domestic Product and the Consumer Confidence Index are obscure terms to those not familiar with the dynamics of the economy.

Still, in every election cycle political candidates intentionally instill confusion and spin the status of the economy to make their economic plans look superior to those of their opponent. The result is an electorate uninformed of the most reliable and descriptive economic indicators. Even worse, continued abuse and distortion of these terms perpetuate a growing sense of racial, economic, and social divisiveness. We have to use the correct language every day in our political discourse, or we will perpetuate label confusion and abuse.

Glossary of Commonly Used Political Terms

Politically Homeless: Voters frustrated with their favorite political party and discouraged by the "politics as usual" from their party leaders and elected officials. Political homelessness can be caused by party leaders and elected officials who intentionally abuse rhetoric and confuse voters with labels, phrases, and made-for-television sound bites. Political homelessness is also caused by party leaders and elected officials who abandon their party's principles and leave their core followers without a "home."

Republican: One of the two major political parties, the Republicans stress less government involvement in individuals' lives and the advocacy of individual achievement. Republicans are generally considered more conservative. In the United States, conservatives usually emphasize free-market economic principles and often prefer state and local governmental power to federal power.

Democrat: One of the two major political parties, the Democrats believe in more government involvement in spending and the advancement of social welfare. Democrats tend to support an activist role for the federal government in the economic and social sectors. The Democratic Party is generally considered to be more liberal or less conservative than the other current major party: the Republican Party.

Independent: In U.S. politics, this term denotes a voter who, when registering to vote, does not declare affiliation with the Republicans, Democrats, or other political parties or does not consider himself or herself to be a member of a political party. Likewise, the term can also refer to a candidate for office who is running on the basis of personal identity rather than party affiliation.

Third Party: In the parlance of American politics, "third party" refers to political parties outside the two-party system that are perceived to have a significant base of support. In the twentieth century, that has come to mean a party that is not the Republican Party or the Democratic Party and can play some role in influencing the outcome of an election.

Conservative: A person who tends to be cautious about new policies or changes in government, who favors traditional values, and who generally feels the government should stay out of the affairs of private citizens and businesses.

Liberal: A person who believes in significant government-managed fiscal and social programs. Liberals believe it is the duty of government to improve social conditions and create a more equitable society. Liberals favor generous spending on the welfare state and believe that poor conditions are a product of social injustices rather than individual failings.

The Great Divides

The polarizing labels and phrases used by our political leaders and elected officials cause confusion over the details of policy issues and contribute to long-term discord between people and groups with opposing political views. This sustained polarization has created three profound divisions throughout our country that I call the great divides. They are the *party divide*, the *racial divide*, and the *economic divide*.

The first great divide is the *party divide*. The party divide is represented by the extreme partisanship that exists between Republicans and Democrats in Washington, D.C., and throughout our country. Three factors have contributed to the growing party divide: differences in party ideology, the political parties' key goals, and the public's apathetic attitude about the activities in the political arena.

The first factor contributing to the party divide is *ideological differences* (see definitions of *Republican* and *Democrat* in the glossary on the previous pages) between the parties concerning the issues most important to the country and the proper solutions needed to address the issues. Ideological differences and healthy debate on the issues go back to the founding of the United States. Our Founding Fathers debated vigorously over the proper size and influence of the central government and the proper role of the United States in the affairs of foreign countries. Two prominent politicians of that time, Alexander Hamilton and Aaron Burr, even settled a dispute with a now-famous duel. Though we no longer settle political disputes with pistols at thirty paces, the current political climate is as divided as any era in our history. A unique characteristic of today's political climate is that we are fighting wars against terror abroad and against our economic infrastructure at home.

We face the reality today that the three pillars of our economic infrastructure—the tax code, Social Security, and

Medicare, which also happen to be the biggest domestic challenges we face—are in danger of collapse. At the same time, we are fighting an enemy abroad who seeks to completely destroy our freedoms and way of life. You should have no doubt in your mind that this is one of the most significant times in our nation's history. The fact that we are confronted by this many critical challenges at one time ensures that we will also face intense debate regarding their proper solutions.

The second factor contributing to the party divide concerns the *goals* of the two major political parties. Both parties want to pass legislation favorable to their overall ideologies and policy agendas. As stated in the introduction, however, neither party has a clear agenda for advocating aggressive policy change. Absent an aggressive agenda, the parties' current goals are often merely winning elections and winning the perceptions war, which is waged with the ammunition of labels, inflammatory rhetoric, and the people's money.

Obviously, a party must win elections to have the opportunity to advocate an aggressive policy agenda. Winning elections only for the sake of victory, however, does not inspire the public to believe change in the status quo is possible. Today we see too many political campaigns fought with personal attacks and deception. Political parties and candidates interested in engaging the public in the political process must inspire the public by explaining the positive effects of aggressive policy change.

An example of deceptive political campaigning is the attack in 2004 by Democratic candidates and Democratic elected officials across the country on the FairTax proposal. The Democratic candidate for U.S. Senate in Georgia released an advertisement in which she says of her Republican opponent, a cosponsor of the FairTax, "He wants a new 23 percent sales tax on nearly everything you buy—cars, groceries, even prescription drugs."

This advertisement is deceptive because it says nothing about the fact that the 23 percent sales tax replaces all federal income taxes or that elimination of the current tax code will increase take-home pay for every employee. Nor does it address the Family Consumption Allowance that will provide monthly payments to offset the cost of necessities like food and prescription drugs, while effectively eliminating the tax burden on the poor, or the fact that the FairTax only applies to purchases of new goods and services. In addition, the candidate offers no plan of her own for reforming or replacing the current tax code.

This political advertisement, like so many others that bombard our televisions every year, discourages the parties and candidates from addressing aggressive policy change. Instead, the object of this and similar advertisements is to "poison the well" by deceiving the public about the facts of the issues. The more you poison the well of political and public discourse, the more people join the ranks of the politically homeless.

The third factor (along with differences in ideology and goals) contributing to the party divide is the public's *political apathy*. A majority of the public is disengaged from the political process, which provides no incentive for the parties and political candidates to change their tactics. Citizens must be proactive in educating themselves on the dynamics of the big issues. An active public, knowledgeable of the issues, would force our elected officials and party leaders to elevate their discourse past personal and sound bite attacks to a discussion on the merits of the issues and their proposed solutions.

The disconnect between the public and the lawmakers causes lawmakers to use rhetoric that appeals to the lowest common denominator of understanding. Politicians feel that an uninformed public cannot understand the minutia of policy details. That is why we so often hear terms like "tax cuts for the rich" or former Democratic vice-presidential candidate John Edwards's continuous complaint that "We live in two Americas." These statements have no basis in fact, but are used to play upon public apathy and ignorance by promoting jealously and economic class warfare.

The second great divide in our country is the *racial divide*. The issue of race and debates surrounding equal rights, protection of rights, and guarantees for all citizens has been a part of our political dialogue since our Founding Fathers penned the Constitution. Today, the issue of race, which includes how various races are affected by policies and predicting how individuals of the various races will cast their votes, continues to permeate our political dialogue and policymaking decisions.

When most political observers write or talk about the role Blacks play in the political arena, their immediate thought or response is likely, "Blacks vote for Democrats." That is a broad, perhaps shallow, but mostly true statement. The history of Black political behavior in terms of voting, especially since 1936, is one of overwhelming support for Democratic candidates at the local, state, and federal levels.

Since 1936, for example, support by Blacks for the Democratic presidential nominee has never dipped below 60 percent. This type of "brand loyalty" is of course desired by, and critical to the success of, Democratic candidates. The almost blind loyalty given by a majority of Blacks to the Democratic Party, however, is a phenomenon that some have equated to the sociological concept of *groupthink*.

Groupthink is a concept described in 1982 by psychologist Irving Janis as "A mode of thinking that people engage in when they are deeply involved in a cohesive in-group, when the members' strivings for unanimity override their motivation to realistically appraise alternative courses of action."

If we want to understand why groupthink exists in the Black electorate, as well as the nature of the racial divides that permeate the current political arena, we must first examine the political players and documents responsible for causing the divides.

In 1896 the U.S. Supreme Court (USSC) established, in the *Plessy v. Ferguson* case, that "separate but equal" facilities, because they were "equal," did not violate the Constitution's Fourteenth Amendment equal protection clause. Justice Henry Billings Brown, writing for the majority, defended "separate but equal" facilities on the grounds that "a distinction which is founded in the color of the two races and which must always exist so long as white men are distinguished from the other race by color—has no tendency to destroy the legal equality of the two races."

Justice Brown further stated, "The object of the [14th] Amendment was undoubtedly to enforce the absolute equality of the two races before the law, but in the nature of things it could not have been intended to abolish distinctions based upon color, or to enforce social, as distinguished from political, equality, or a commingling of the two races upon terms unsatisfactory to either."

The USSC decision in *Plessy* was not unanimous. Justice John Marshall Harlan, who ultimately wrote the correct opinion, was the lone dissenter. He did not see in the Constitution a justification to view citizens differently based on race. Justice Harlan wrote in his dissent,

> But in view of the Constitution, in the eye of the law, there is in this country no superior, dominant, ruling class of citizens. There is no caste here. Our Constitution is color-blind, and neither knows nor tolerates classes among citizens. In respect of civil rights, all citizens are equal before the law. The humblest is the peer of the most powerful. The law regards man as man, and takes no account of his surroundings or of his color when his civil rights as guaranteed by the supreme law of the land are involved. It is, therefore, to be regretted that this high tribunal, the final expositor of the fundamental law of the land, has reached the conclusion that it is

competent for a State to regulate the enjoyment by
citizens of their civil rights solely upon the basis of
race.

With its ruling on the *Plessy* case, the USSC embarked on a
slippery slope that would lead future courts and lawmaking
bodies to view citizens as members of a particular race, requiring equal protection of the laws because of their race, instead of
as individual citizens who are guaranteed equal protection of
the laws because of the Fourteenth Amendment's mandate.

The "separate but equal" doctrine stood until 1954, when
the USSC struck down, in the *Brown v. Board of Education* case,
"separate but equal" facilities. In the Brown opinion, Chief
Justice Earl Warren stated that,

> . . . to separate (school children) solely because of
> their race generates a feeling of inferiority as to their
> status in the community that may affect their hearts
> and minds in a way unlikely ever to be undone. . . .
> Whatever may have been the extent of psychological
> knowledge at the time of *Plessy v. Ferguson*, this
> finding is amply supported by modern authority. Any
> language in *Plessy v. Ferguson* to this finding is
> rejected. We conclude that in the field of public
> education the doctrine of "separate but equal" has no
> place. Separate educational facilities are inherently
> unequal.

The glaring omission in the *Brown* opinion is that Warren did
not cite Justice Harlan's dissenting opinion from *Plessy*. Warren
could have written that *Brown* overruled *Plessy* strictly on the
basis of the Fourteenth Amendment's equal protection clause,
thereby validating Harlan's argument that the Constitution is
colorblind. Instead, with its decision in *Brown*, the USSC still
refused to support the Fourteenth Amendment based on a strict
reading of its language.

Fourteenth Amendment to the Constitution

Section 1. All persons born or naturalized in the United States, and subject to the jurisdiction thereof, are citizens of the United States and of the state wherein they reside. No state shall make or enforce any law which shall abridge the privileges or immunities of citizens of the United States; nor shall any state deprive any person of life, liberty, or property, without due process of law; nor deny to any person within its jurisdiction the equal protection of the laws.

Warren's court was certainly correct in overturning the *Plessy* decision. His broad, liberal justification, however, laid the groundwork for future court rulings and laws that viewed citizens not as equal individuals, but as members of various racial groups in need of special protections.

Indeed, Congress passed a number of landmark laws in the years following the *Brown* decision that addressed many of the inequities and discriminations racial minorities faced. The Civil Rights Act of 1957, passed during the Eisenhower administration, established the Civil Rights Section of the U.S. Justice Department and allowed federal prosecutors to obtain court injunctions against individuals who interfered with others' voting rights.

The Civil Rights Act of 1964, passed during President Lyndon Johnson's administration, prohibited discrimination in public facilities, in government, in employment, and created the Equal Employment Opportunities Commission. The act made it illegal to compel racial segregation in schools, housing, or in hiring practices.

The act not only opened many doors for Blacks and other racial minorities, it also provided the impetus for the feminist movement and later programs such as affirmative action. The Civil Rights Act of 1964 was of course controversial at the time of its passage, and many Southern Democrats in Congress opposed it. Its passage, however, brought the nation closer to the Founders' vision of "equal protection of the laws" for all citizens.

Unfortunately, President Johnson was not content with legislation that, to him, merely made discriminatory practices illegal and sought to treat all citizens equally regardless of race or ethnicity. In his 1965 commencement address at Howard University, Johnson permanently muddied the waters of race relations and treatment of racial minorities by the courts, the law, and government and private institutions. In the section of his remarks titled "Freedom Is Not Enough," President Johnson stated,

> It is not enough just to open the gates of opportunity. All our citizens must have the ability to walk through those gates. This is the next and the more profound stage of the battle for civil rights. We seek not just freedom but opportunity. We seek not just legal equity but human ability, not just equality as a right and a theory but equality as a fact and equality as a result. To this end equal opportunity is essential, but not enough.

President Johnson went on to say, "Perhaps most important—its influence radiating to every part of life—is the breakdown of the Negro family structure. For this, most of all, White America must accept responsibility."

With his speech to Howard University, and the affirmative action and quota laws that were subsequently passed, Blacks were no longer viewed as individuals in the eyes of federal and state courts, nor in the eyes of Congress, nor in the eyes of the White Democrat elites, nor in the eyes of the soon-to-emerge, self-appointed Black leaders.

The question central to an examination of the opinions in *Plessy* and *Brown*, of the Civil Rights Acts of 1957 and 1964, and of President Johnson's Howard University commencement speech is "Do Constitutional rights and guarantees belong to classes and races, or to individuals?" Chief Justice Warren stated in his opinion in *Brown* that the intentions of the Founding Fathers "are inconclusive." Yet the language of the Fourteenth Amendment could not be clearer. What part of "No state shall . . . deny to *any person* within its jurisdiction the equal protection of the laws" did Warren and others not understand? Our Founding Founders knew a nation that viewed and treated its citizens as individuals would be constrained from dividing them and treating them inequitably. The emergence of Black groupthink is the unfortunate product of our courts and laws treating Blacks as a monolithic group instead of as individual citizens.

Another factor responsible for perpetuating Black groupthink was the subsequent emergence of the so-called Black leaders who successfully convinced the majority of Blacks that their economic prosperity and survival was dependent upon their support of the Democratic Party and its liberal economic and social policy agendas. The so-called Black leaders are activists like Jesse Jackson, Al Sharpton, and Joseph Lowery, along with NAACP Chairman Julian Bond and numerous Black elected officials across the country. These "leaders" have for decades preached to the Black electorate the myth that their prospects for success are wholly contingent on Blacks voting as a bloc for Democrat candidates, regardless of the candidates' race, and on their active support for liberal policies. I refer to these individuals as the "so-called Black leaders" because I do not in my lifetime recall an election in which Blacks got together to select *our* leaders. Nor do I recall anyone appointing them leaders of all Blacks. The last time I checked, I am a citizen of the United States, and the Black citizens have not seceded from the Union.

The so-called Black leaders rose to prominence in the political arena due to their activism in the 1960s on behalf of the civil rights and voting rights struggles. Many were schooled under the tutelage of Dr. Martin Luther King, Jr. No one can deny them the honor in fighting for and securing basic civil and voting rights for all citizens. Unfortunately, many of those, like Jesse Jackson and Joseph Lowery, who fought so long and hard to achieve a society and system of laws blind to the color of one's skin, have fought even harder in the years since to keep Blacks on the Democrat plantation and make race a key component of discussion on virtually all political issues.

The so-called Black leaders want to remain atop the lofty perch of notoriety and success, but to do so they must have support from a majority of the Black electorate. The formula for maintaining their prominence and power is quite simple: Convince the White Democratic Party leaders that they can deliver a majority of votes from Blacks, and the Democratic establishment rewards them monetarily and publicly. Because the "leaders" have their entire lives invested in maintaining power and influence over the Black electorate, while at the same time reaping vast financial rewards, they seek to impose harsh and public sanctions on any African-American who dares leave or criticize their Democratic plantation.

We have all heard the terms used to vilify Black Republicans: "token Black," "Uncle Tom," "sellout," and some that cannot even be printed here. Yes, I have been called some of these labels, but I am unfazed by anyone who would deny my Constitutional and God-given right to *think* and *decide* for myself. Prominent African-Americans in President Bush's cabinet, including former Secretary of State Colin Powell, current Secretary of State Condoleezza Rice, and former Secretary of Education Rod Paige, as well as Supreme Court Justice Clarence Thomas, have all been criticized simply because they worked for or were nominated by a Republican administration.

I was criticized by a so-called Black leader in 2004 for running in the Georgia Senate Primary race as a Republican (see text box on following page). I was not surprised or disturbed by the criticism. Rev. Joseph Lowery, former president of the Southern Christian Leadership Conference, criticized the fact

"Senate Candidates Court Black Officials"

Lowery warmed up the 100 or so people in attendance by bashing Republicans in general and President Bush and former President Ronald Reagan in particular. Lowery then alluded to a recent conversation he said he had with former Godfather's Pizza CEO Herman Cain, the only African-American seeking the Republican nod for [U.S. Senator Zell] Miller's job. Cain is a strong conservative and unapologetic backer of Bush. Cain also has been reaching out to Democratic black voters, hoping they will cross over and vote for him in the July 20 primary.

"You're black as you can be," Lowery recalled that he told Cain during a telephone conversation. "But if you're a Bush-Reagan Republican, you cannot get my vote." Lowery then went a step further. He said he would like nothing better than to campaign for a "black man" running for the U.S. Senate. He paused, grinned, looked out over the audience toward [Democrat U.S. Senate candidate Denise] Majette, and said enthusiastically: "But I guess I'll have to settle for a black woman."

The crowd burst into applause for the only African-American seeking the Democratic nomination as Majette smiled and acknowledged Lowery's support. Lowery had few kind words for black Republicans. "There's a myth going around that to be rich and famous you have to be Republican," he said. "And some colored folks are falling for that. No black people, but some colored folks."

Source: Jim Tharpe, *The Atlanta Journal-Constitution*, 27 June 2004.

that I was running as a Republican for U.S. Senate at a lunch hosted by the Georgia Association of Black Elected Officials.

Lowery used the phrases "colored people" and "black people" in his speech to attack me and attempt to scare other

Blacks who may be conservative and Republican from leaving the Democratic plantation. He used this racially divisive language to remind Black people in the audience of the days of segregation—the days when coloreds had to eat, drink, and sleep in separate facilities. To Lowery and the other so-called Black leaders, "colored" is a derogatory term that equates conservative Blacks with the whites responsible for segregation.

It is sad that the same people who literally poured their blood, sweat, and tears into the fight for equal opportunity for all races now lead the most vociferous attacks against Blacks who dare rise to the most respected levels of government or achieve success in the business world as members of the Republican Party. It is at the same time illustrative of the fact that today's so-called Black leaders do not work to provide better futures for those they claim to represent. Rather, their goal is to control as many of the votes from the Black electorate as possible, which ensures that their positions of power and influence remain safe.

Followers of the so-called Black leaders and advocates of their social policies should take a close look at the statistics on Black economic and social performance. According to Census 2002, home ownership among Whites was 71 percent, 5 percent higher than the national rate of 66 percent. In contrast, homeownership among Blacks was 46 percent, 20 percent below the national average. At the same time, the national poverty rate was 11.7 percent. The poverty rate for Blacks, however, was 22.7 percent, while only 7.8 percent of Whites were below the poverty level.

According to the Centers for Disease Control and Prevention (CDCP), the abortion ratio for Black women (503 per 1,000 live births) is three times the ratio for white women (167 per 1,000 live births), and Black women have 32 percent of all abortions while the Black population is only 12 percent of this nation. In addition, the CDCP reports that in 2002, 68.6

percent of Black children were born out of wedlock. Yes! Nearly 70 percent, and this is not a typing error.

These statistics illustrate the hollowness in forty years of promises by the so-called Black leaders that the policies of the Democratic Party would lift all Blacks from poverty and oppression. In following these pied pipers, Blacks have severely limited their opportunities for economic success because for too long they have looked at themselves as a group first and individuals second.

Not all prominent Black leaders have followed the negative and divisive groupthink model employed by the likes of Jesse Jackson, Al Sharpton, and Joseph Lowery. Dr. Martin Luther King Jr., whom many consider a Founding Father in the struggle to end discrimination and ensure equal opportunities for all citizens, inspired people and led with the idea that change could occur through grassroots mobilization and positive negotiation with political and business leaders. Dr. King's positive leadership created the impetus for aggressive social change and is the reason why Americans of every racial background revere him today.

Another positive leader is Washington, D.C. mayor Anthony Williams. Mayor Williams in 2003 helped initiate a system to provide more than one thousand vouchers per year to poor children in the failing Washington, D.C. public school system. The voucher system is called the "District of Columbia Opportunity Scholarship Program," and it allows students from financially troubled homes to attend private schools in the D.C. area. Mayor Williams has of course received the expected outrage and criticism from the teachers' unions and so-called Black leaders like D.C. congressional delegate Eleanor Holmes Norton, but he knows that education and doing all he can to provide a better future for D.C.'s children is more important than politics.

I also must mention Andrew Young, a pioneer with Dr. King in the fight for civil rights and equal opportunities and a former mayor of Atlanta, U.S. congressman, and U.S. ambassador. Mr.

Young has told me more than once, "Black people have to learn how to be bipartisan. We don't have a permanent party. We have permanent issues and interests."

Fortunately, encouraging trends are emerging in the Black electorate. More and more Blacks are realizing that the road to personal economic security does not go through the Democratic Party or another big government social program. The Joint Center for Political and Economic Studies found in its 2004 National Opinion Poll that more Blacks than ever are

---

Joint Center for Political and Economic Studies 2004 National Opinion Poll Key Findings

Blacks in age brackets twenty-six years old and over identify themselves with the Democratic Party on average 16 percent less than in 2000. Self-identification as *Independent* has risen in all age brackets for blacks aged thirty-six years old and over by an average of 7 percent, and identification with the *Republican* Party since 2000 has risen by an average of 3 percent.

Other encouraging statistics show that 18 percent of Blacks polled plan to vote for Republican President George W. Bush, which is double the percentage in 2000. The numbers are even better for self-identified *secular* or *Christian* conservative blacks. 29 and 36 percent of blacks in those groups, respectively, plan to vote for President Bush, which is triple the percentage from the 2000 election.

Despite the barrage of bad economic news we hear daily from the media, 60 percent of Blacks surveyed in the Joint Center's poll said they are financially the same or better off than a year ago. The statistic perhaps most telling that Blacks are ready to "leave the Democrat plantation" and look for new solutions is that Jesse Jackson's *favorable* rating dropped from 83 percent in the 2000 poll to 58 percent in the 2004 poll.

indicating a desire to support Republican candidates and identify themselves as Independent or Republican.

The statistics listed in the text box on the following page show that a significant percentage of Blacks are beginning to see past the decades-old negative perceptions about the Republican Party and the conservative political ideology. They are moving from *rhetoric* to *reality*; from *groupthink* to *you think*. Individual Blacks are questioning the logic behind continuing to believe in the same leaders, lawmakers, and policies when conditions for many Blacks have stayed the same for years or become even worse.

Due to the influence of Black churches, the political views of most Blacks are more conservative than they realize. Studies show that most Blacks are opposed to same-sex marriage, are eager to curtail the high Black abortion rate, and anxious to reform the big economic issues that have a disproportionately negative effect on Blacks. Conservative values and ideologies on social and fiscal issues are a natural home for Blacks.

Blacks can no longer look at conservative Supreme Court Justice Clarence Thomas as an outlier or aberration. In the recent past we have seen the rise of many successful conservative Blacks, such as the aforementioned Colin Powell, Condoleezza Rice, and Rod Paige, as well as Secretary of Housing and Urban Development Alphonso Jackson, former FCC Chairman Michael Powell, Maryland Lt. Governor Michael Steele, Ohio Secretary of State Ken Blackwell, Texas Energy Commissioner Michael Williams, political and economic commentators Thomas Sowell, Star Parker, Rev. Jesse Lee Peterson, and Walter Williams, and scores of others throughout the business world and state and local politics. The common denominator of all the aforementioned great Black Americans is that they think for themselves. That's the result of knowing the facts and understanding the history of the political parties.

In the late 1800s, Booker T. Washington, founder of Tuskegee Institute and the first Black ever to dine at the White House with the president, envisioned Black self-reliance when he stated that a Black citizen "should acquire property, own his own land, drive his own mule hitched to his own wagon, milk his own cow, raise his own crop, and keep out of debt, and when he acquired a home he became fit for a conservative citizen." Booker T. Washington's vision is for the same "Ownership Society" President Bush talks about today . . . one hundred years later.

Blacks have been told by their so-called leaders that the Republican Party is the home of "rich white guys" and that conservatism is inherently racist. Thus, the majority of Blacks over time have come to perceive all political issues through the lens of race. They see race as the root of all issues and the cause of all their problems. In reality, conservative policies are colorblind. For example, a tax code and regulatory policies that unburden small businesses, allow them to grow and hire more employees, and allow owners to pass these businesses on to their heirs benefit all small business owners regardless of race.

Of course, Blacks and the so-called Black leaders cannot shoulder all the blame for sharing the perception that the Republican Party does not speak to them or their economic and social values. The Republicans have done a poor job of reaching out to Blacks and educating them on the realities of conservative economic and social policies. The Democrats have surely taken their support among Blacks for granted, but Republicans until recently have been content to let the Democrats keep that support.

Many Republicans scratch their heads and wonder aloud why Blacks would continue to support a party that has betrayed them and taken them for granted for more than fifty years. These same Republicans should not be surprised that Blacks generally vote as a bloc, because both parties have treated Blacks as a separate bloc for more than one hundred years! The conversion of a relative minority of Blacks to the Republican Party should be seen as an example of many Blacks reaching in instead of the party reaching out.

Many people involved in the Republican Party leadership at the national and state levels are still tied to the good-old-boy, country club style of politics that determines which candidates will represent their party based on "Whose turn is it?" and "Who has paid their dues?" This is the perception of the Republican Party among a majority of Blacks. Whether it is the truth or not is irrelevant, just as it is irrelevant if Republicans are upset when Democrats accuse them of "cutting Social Security." Perception is reality in politics, and perception remains reality until drastic efforts in the form of long-term, strategic plans are made to educate the public on the facts.

We must remember that the majority of Blacks prior to the Great Depression primarily supported Republican candidates. Only after presidents such as Franklin Roosevelt and Lyndon Johnson reached out to Blacks through their rhetoric and policy agendas did the Black electorate move steadily to the ideological left. To win back the votes and support of Blacks in large numbers, Republicans must demonstrate and properly communicate that their policies and ideology are more in line with economic and social values held by most Blacks. In the long run, facts will triumph over rhetoric. The race to win back the votes of Blacks is a marathon, not a sprint.

The third great divide in our country is the *economic divide*, which starts with education. Slightly more than forty years ago Congress passed, and President Johnson signed into law, the Civil Rights Act of 1964. Since that time, thousands of Blacks have attained a college education, achieved financial success, started their own businesses, and risen to the highest levels of the corporate and political arenas. The long struggle to achieve equal opportunities for success in nearly all facets of our society has reaped great rewards for all U.S. citizens. Much of Dr. King's dream of equal opportunity for all citizens to achieve success is more possible than ever before, but many Blacks have not yet seized their full potential through the education and economic systems. It starts with personal responsibility and motivation, not the government.

For nearly every citizen, attainment of a quality education is an absolute minimum requirement for success in life, whether you measure success by economic status or virtually any other standard. Yet, after forty years of desegregated schools and the guarantees written in the Civil Rights Act, some Blacks still lag behind Whites in measures of educational and economic achievement.

National Center for Education Studies
Key Statistics on Measures of Educational Achievement

The National Adult Literacy Survey found that 38 to 43 percent of Black adults scored in the lowest level on tests designed to measure literacy skills, compared to 14 to 16 percent of Whites.

In 2001, 11 percent of 16- to 24-year-olds dropped out of high school across the nation. The dropout rate for Whites was 7 percent, the rate for Blacks was 11 percent, and Hispanics had a dropout rate of 27 percent.

87 percent of Blacks aged 25 to 29 years old have completed high school, versus a 93 percent completion rate among Whites.

Blacks were conferred 9 percent of all Bachelor's degrees, 8 percent of all Master's degrees, and 5 percent of all Doctoral degrees. Whites were conferred 71 percent of Bachelor's degrees, 62 percent of Master's degrees, and 57 percent of Doctoral degrees

Let's be clear about the reference to statistics here and throughout this book. Statistics represent a static aggregate measurement. They represent a reference point from which to develop concepts, policies, and practices intended to move the "epicenter" toward improvement.

No one doubts that academic achievement is a prerequisite for achieving economic freedom. In fact, I believe that if Dr. King were alive today, his focus would be on encouraging Blacks to close the academic achievement gap with Whites as a precursor to achieving economic success. Closing the academic achievement gap and achieving economic freedom, though, cannot be done with more federal government social and tax policies that discourage self-reliance and redistribute wealth to minority communities.

Black families must bear more of the burden for encouraging their children to achieve academic success. There are too many negative influences and peer pressures today among Blacks associated with academic achievement. Too many Blacks, however, will not admit that there is a problem. In March 2004, Dr. Bill Cosby, the well-known actor and comedian, stunned and angered the NAACP when he stated in an address to that organization,

> Ladies and gentlemen, the lower economic people are not holding up their end in this deal. These people are not parenting. They are buying things for kids— $500 sneakers for what? And won't spend $200 for "Hooked on Phonics." They're standing on the corner and they can't speak English. I can't even talk the way these people talk: "Why you ain't," "Where you is . . . ." And I blamed the kid until I heard the mother talk. And then I heard the father talk. . . . Everybody knows it's important to speak English except these knuckleheads. . . . You can't be a doctor with that kind of crap coming out of your mouth!

The truth sometimes hurts. In this case some people were offended. That's too bad! Bill Cosby had the personal podium of his success to "tell it like it is," and I am glad he did.

One of the strongest aspects of President Bush's No Child Left Behind (NCLB) legislation is that it places a greater emphasis on achievement at the early stages of education. What it does not emphasize, however, is greater parental involvement. When the president, every elected official, and every teacher discuss NCLB, they should mention the necessity of parental involvement in the education of children. Although not practical for the title of an initiative, No Child Left Behind *with* Parental Involvement would stress the point.

I do agree with those who argue that evaluating all schools based on one testing score is the wrong approach for finding whether or not a school is passing or failing. There are too many different dynamics between schools that play a role in determining academic achievement. The biggest complaint, however, among teachers and administrators I meet is that many children do not come to school anxious and eager to learn. These children are not encouraged to learn at home, so they do not see education as the means to success later in life.

In addition to encouraging a greater level of parental involvement in education, we must move beyond politics and rhetoric and teach our children, as well as many adults, the facts of our economic system. I call it elementary economics. Too many of our citizens are uninformed about the negative effects of the onerous tax code, about who actually pays taxes in our country, and about the dynamics involved in job creation.

The blame partially falls on liberal politicians who for many decades have misled citizens about the facts of basic economics while promoting a political structure based on jealousy and class warfare. The blame also falls on our educational system for failing to teach the basic dynamics of our market-based economic system, and on the apathetic percentage of the public that appears content to allow the government to tax them when they are not looking and then accuses the so-called "rich" for causing their economic situation.

Liberal politicians have also misled people about who actually pays most of the taxes in this country. One of their favorite promises is to provide a tax cut for the middle class. *I have a breaking announcement—There is no middle class!*

Who pays taxes in the United States?

• Top 1 percent of income earners pay 32 percent of all income taxes

• Top 5 percent of income earners pay 51 percent of all income taxes

• Top 10 percent of income earners pay 64 percent of all income taxes

• Top 20 percent of income earners pay 78 percent of all income taxes

• *Bottom 80 percent of income earners pay 20 percent of all income taxes*

Source: Congressional Budget Office report, *Effective Tax Rates Under Law, 2001 to 2014*

The statistics in the chart above show that *20 percent of income earners in the nation pay nearly 80 percent of all income taxes.* Where is this middle class the Democrats keep talking about? Yet we never hear an end to the liberal chorus that cuts in the tax rates are "tax cuts for the rich." Liberals believe that the amount of control they can exert over your life is directly related to the amount of taxes they can take from your paycheck.

A favorite tactic of liberals is to instill among the bottom 80 percent of wage earners who only pay 20 percent of all income taxes the belief that tax cuts are only going to the rich. Who is this "rich" 20 percent who shoulder the majority of the tax

burden? The top 20 percent of income earners are those who
have average yearly earnings of just over $180,000. The top 40
percent of income earners have average yearly earnings of just
over $75,000. Many of these "rich" people are small business
owners who employ the majority of other wage earners in our
country. Most of them would laugh at you if you called them
"rich."

Virtually every decision individuals and businesses make
about their futures is in some way related to the amount of
money they have to spend. The more of your own money you
get to keep determines the amount of control exerted over you
by the federal government. The less control the federal government has over your life, the closer you are to achieving
economic freedom.

It is no wonder, then, why the facts about the tax code and
who actually pays taxes in our country are obscured and
manipulated by politicians whose political futures depend on
control of the economy and the process of taxation.

Just as the so-called Black leaders have instilled the
groupthink mentality into a large percentage of the Black
population, liberal leaders in Congress have attempted to instill
a class warfare mentality in all citizens at the lowest levels of
educational and economic achievement. The result is that
instead of blaming Congress for enacting wrongheaded policies
that discourage achievement, many of the uneducated and poor
blame the rich for causing their lack of success.

The only way liberalism can survive as a viable policy
alternative for the Democratic Party is if the citizens of this
country continue to view themselves as members of downtrod-
den groups whose only hope for survival is more assistance
from the federal government. The great irony, of course, is that
liberal policies cause people to view themselves as members
of groups and create the barriers that discourage educational
attainment and economic freedom! The proponents of

liberalism know this, but they hope a lot of people will never figure it out.

The good news is that a lot of people *have* figured it out. Conservatives know that the real path to success lies in the combination of education, individual initiative, and a federal government that is in the business of removing barriers to success.

Abraham Lincoln said, "You don't help the poor by hurting the rich." I might add that you help the poor by helping everybody.

It's Time to Wake Up!

I believe that the three great divides—the *party divide*, the *racial divide*, and the *economic divide*—polarize our nation. The liberal political ideology seeks to enact policies that divide us and attempts to control all aspects of society and all facets of our lives. If you think that sounds a lot like the tried-and-failed government systems of socialism and communism, you are correct.

The liberal, socialist ideology cannot exist among a society educated on the detrimental facts of liberal policies and the dynamics of elementary economics. That is why liberal politicians seek to herd the public into groups and pit those groups against each other, as if as citizens of the United States we do not all share the dream of educational and economic success. Liberal politicians do not share your dreams of success because your success and the success of your children and grandchildren spell the end to their reign of power over your life.

Many citizens have come to believe that as Americans they do not have to shoulder the responsibilities of individual achievement and participation in the political arena. For too many years, liberals have usurped our individual responsibilities and made our most important decisions for us. By ceding responsibility, however, we have paid a price, and that price is the erosion of our freedoms.

As citizens of this great nation, we can no longer allow the federal government to treat Blacks and other minority groups as mere members of groups and to constantly erect barriers to individual achievement. God did not create each of us in His image so we could lead lives of constant leisure as a group, riddled with a "blame-everyone-else" attitude for our circumstances. Every individual citizen possesses within the potential for individual attainment of success. It is up to us to reclaim our government and the decision-making processes that affect nearly every aspect of our lives.

The party divide will be closed when the public ends its apathy toward the activities in the political arena, educates itself on the facts of our biggest economic and social issues, and works to elect political leaders who share these beliefs. Only then will our political leaders and political candidates stop talking down to the public with sound-bite rhetoric and start speaking in facts.

The racial divide will be closed when individual Blacks realize that their success and the future success of their children depend on individual achievement in the education and economic arenas. Only then will Blacks be able to throw off the shackles of groupthink imposed on them by their own so-called Black leaders.

The economic divide will be closed with education and when parents take a greater interest and role in the education of their children. We must create a culture that makes academic achievement and excellence possible for all of our children. Nearly every child has the ability to learn and turn his or her education into a successful career.

Wake up, America! For the sake of our country, our government, and our children's and grandchildren's future.

Politically Homeless

Labels and Empty Rhetoric

- The politically homeless are voters frustrated with their favorite political party or discouraged by what they see as "politics as usual." Some of the politically homeless choose to stay with their party out of a sense of principle or tradition, but they do not actively identify with the party.
- A key contributor to political homelessness is the confusion caused, often intentionally, by the seemingly never-ending barrage of labels, phrases, and made-for-television sound bites we hear every day from our elected officials.

The Great Divides

- The polarizing labels and phrases used by our political leaders and elected officials have created three profound divisions throughout our country. I call these the *party divide*, the *racial divide*, and the *economic divide*.
- The *party divide* is represented by the extreme partisanship that exists between Republicans and Democrats in Washington, D.C. and throughout our country.
- The second great divide in our country is the *racial divide*. Race is often abused by candidates and so-called Black leaders to keep voters neatly on their respective plantations.
- The third great divide in our country is the *economic divide*. Economics starts with education. The long struggle to achieve equal opportunities for success in nearly all facets of our society has resulted in great progress for all citizens.

It's Time to Wake Up!

- The *party divide* will be closed when the public ends its apathy toward the activities in the political arena, educates itself on the facts of our biggest economic and social issues, and works to elect political leaders who share these beliefs.
- The *racial divide* will be closed when individual Blacks are able to throw off the shackles of groupthink imposed on them by their so-called Black leaders.
- The *economic divide* will be closed with education and when parents take a greater interest and role in the education of their children.

Chapter Three

Voters Are Not as Dumb as Democrats Think

Many of the politically homeless found temporary shelter in the Republican Party on election day in 2004 when they cast their votes in support of the conservative policy agenda. Conservative Democrats, conservative Christians, members of other religious, racial, and ethnic backgrounds, and millions across the entire nation who have never before registered or voted cast their ballots for Republican candidates who promise to continue to prosecute the global war on terrorism, pursue aggressive policy solutions to our biggest economic issues, and escalate the battle to protect our nation's moral foundations. The Democratic Party, for many decades the political home for a majority of Americans, is now a party in search of a voice to define its message and direct its future.

History Is Not on the Democrats' Side

Even though Democrats claim to be the party that champions civil rights, history and the facts are not on their side. The Democratic Party formed the Ku Klux Klan in the 1800s to terrorize and lynch Blacks who dared register to vote or vote for Republican candidates. Democrats have successfully co-opted credit for passing landmark civil rights legislation because President Lyndon Johnson signed two major acts into law. A closer look at the facts, however, reveals that historically members of the Democratic Party have served as a barrier to providing equal opportunities for all citizens.

All of the landmark legislation detailed in the following table was accomplished under Republican presidents with Republican congressional leadership, except for the two acts actually signed by President Lyndon Johnson. Even then, it was the Republicans in Congress that pushed for passage and voted for the legislation at a higher percentage than the congressional Democrats. In every case, Democrats fought the hardest to deny the civil rights of the voters they now take for granted.

Important Federal Activity and Legislation on Civil Rights: 1858–1965

1858: Abraham Lincoln delivered his "House Divided" speech to the Illinois Republican State Convention. Regarding the issue of slavery, Lincoln stated, "A house divided against itself cannot stand. I believe this government cannot endure permanently half slave and half free. I do not expect the Union to be dissolved—I do not expect the house to fall—but I do expect it will cease to be divided."

1860: Abraham Lincoln was elected sixteenth president of the United States. In his January 1861 Inaugural Address,

Lincoln sent this warning to the Southern slave-owning states: "In your hands, my dissatisfied fellow country-men, and not in mine, is the momentous issue of civil war . . . . You have no oath registered in Heaven to destroy the government, while I shall have the most solemn one to preserve, protect, and defend it."

1863: President Lincoln issued the Emancipation Proclamation, which declared that "all persons held as slaves within any State or designated part of a State . . . shall be then, thenceforward, and forever free." The Emancipation Proclamation did not immediately free a single slave, but from January 1, 1863, and on, every advance of Union troops in the Civil War expanded the cause of freedom.

In his famous "I Have A Dream" speech, Dr. Martin Luther King Jr. said of Lincoln and the Proclamation, "Five score years ago, a great American, in whose symbolic shadow we stand, signed the Emancipation Proclamation. This momentous decree came as a great beacon light of hope to millions of Negro slaves who had been seared in the flames of withering injustice. It came as a joyous daybreak to end the long night of captivity."

1865: The Thirteenth Amendment to the U.S. Constitution was ratified. The Thirteenth Amendment states, "Neither slavery nor involuntary servitude, except as a punish-ment for crime whereof the party shall have been duly convicted, shall exist within the United States, or any place subject to their jurisdiction."

Congress approved the Amendment to abolish slavery in all of the United States. Once the Confederate states were defeated, approval of the Thirteenth Amendment was required for readmittance into the United States.

1868: The Fourteenth Amendment to the U.S. Constitution was ratified. The Fourteenth Amendment states, in part, "All persons born or naturalized in the United States, and subject to the jurisdiction thereof, are citizens of the United States and of the state wherein they reside. No state shall make or enforce any law which shall abridge the privileges or immunities of citizens of the United States; nor shall any state deprive any person of life, liberty, or property, without due process of law; nor deny to any person within its jurisdiction the equal protection of the laws."

The amendment ensured that all former slaves were granted automatic United States citizenship and that they would have all the rights and privileges of any other citizen.

1870: The Fifteenth Amendment to the U.S. Constitution was ratified. The Fifteenth Amendment states, "The right of citizens of the United States to vote shall not be denied or abridged by the United States or by any State on account of race, color, or previous condition of servitude."

The amendment sought to ensure that a person's race, color, or prior history as a slave would not be used to bar that person from voting.

1954: With its ruling in *Brown v. Board of Education*, the United States Supreme Court struck down "separate but equal" facilities for Whites and Blacks.

1957: As a result of the *Brown v. Board of Education* ruling, nine African-American students enrolled at Central High School in Little Rock, Arkansas. Arkansas Governor Orval Faubus defied the *Brown* ruling and called in the Arkansas National Guard to prevent the students— dubbed the "Little Rock Nine"—from entering the school building. Ten days later in a meeting with President Eisenhower, Governor Faubus agreed to use the National Guard to protect the students. Upon returning to Little Rock, however, he dismissed the troops, leaving the students exposed to an angry White mob. When Governor Faubus failed to restore order, President Eisenhower dispatched 101st Airborne Division paratroopers to Little Rock and put the Arkansas National Guard under federal command. Under federal protection, the "Little Rock Nine" finished out the school year. The following year, Governor Faubus closed all the high schools, forcing the African-American students to take correspondence courses or go to out-of-state schools.

1957: President Dwight Eisenhower sent to Congress legislation to address civil rights violations. Congress later passed, and President Eisenhower signed into law, the Civil Rights Act of 1957, the first civil rights legislation enacted since Reconstruction. Congressional Democrats substantially weakened the final version of the act. The act established the Civil Rights Section of the Justice Department and empowered federal prosecutors to obtain court injunctions against interference with the right to vote. The act also established a federal Civil Rights Commission with authority to investigate discriminatory conditions and recommend corrective measures.

1960: President Eisenhower signed into law a second civil
rights bill. The 1960 act extends the life of the Civil
Rights Commission, introduces new penalties against
anyone who obstructs someone's attempt to vote or
register to vote, and gives the U.S. attorney general the
power to inspect state and local voting records in
elections for U.S. Government offices. Like the 1957
act, the 1960 act was greatly weakened by Southern
congressional Democrats before it was sent to
President Eisenhower.

1964: The Twenty-fourth Amendment to the U.S. Constitution
was ratified. The Twenty-fourth Amendment states,
"The right of citizens of the United States to vote in any
primary or other election for President or Vice
President, for electors for President or Vice President, or
for Senator or Representative in Congress, shall not be
denied or abridged by the United States or any State by
reason of failure to pay any poll tax or other tax."
Prior to ratification of the Twenty-fourth
Amendment, several Southern states sought to bar or
discourage Blacks from participating in elections by
requiring all voters to pay a tax before they could vote.

1964: President Lyndon Johnson signed into law the Civil
Rights Act of 1964. The 1964 act is landmark legislation
that prohibited discrimination in public facilities, in
government, and in employment and created the Equal
Employment Opportunities Commission. The act made it
illegal to compel racial segregation in schools, in
housing, or in hiring practices. Like the 1957 and 1960
acts, the 1964 act was vehemently opposed by
Southern Democrats.

> **1965:** President Johnson signed into law the Voting Rights Act of 1965. The act empowered the federal government to oversee voter registration and elections in counties that had used tests to determine voter eligibility. Soon after its passage, Black voter registration greatly increased. The act was extended in 1970, 1975, and 1982 and has restored the right to vote guaranteed by the Constitution's Fourteenth and Fifteenth Amendments.

After signing the Civil Rights Act of 1964, President Lyndon Johnson congratulated congressional Republicans for their overwhelming support. It was Illinois Republican senator Everett Dirksen who gathered support in the U.S. Senate to block the Democrats' months-long filibuster against the act. In response to a question regarding the reasons for his dedication to civil rights legislation, Senator Dirksen stated, "I am involved in mankind, and whatever the skin, we are all included in mankind."

Following passage of the 1964 act, NAACP chairman Roy Wilkins awarded Senator Dirksen the Leadership Conference of Civil Rights Award for the senator's "remarkable civil rights leadership."

The previous timeline illustrates that history is clearly on the side of the Republicans. Republican presidents, senators, and representatives are responsible for enacting the most important pieces of civil rights legislation in our nation's history.

President George W. Bush made history in the 2004 presidential race by receiving the most votes ever cast for a presidential candidate. Bush also increased his electoral vote count from the 2000 election, from 271 to 286 electoral votes. Not since President Reagan's 1984 victory, which set the record for most electoral votes won in a presidential election, has a candidate won such a clear majority of the states in the South and the West.

The 2004 elections were significant for a number of reasons. First, the majority of voters stated that they based their presidential vote on moral issues, which include opposition to same-sex marriage initiatives and partial-birth abortion and support for confirmation of conservative federal judges. The issue most political pundits assumed would be paramount in people's minds when they cast their vote, the global war on terrorism, was cited by voters as the third most important factor.

Second, President Bush received a majority of the vote among Catholic and Protestant voters and increased his percentage of support among a number of other demographic groups, including members of racial minorities and voters who live in urban areas (see following table).

Third, the U.S. electorate sent to Congress a "working majority" of Republicans in the U.S. House and Senate. Republicans increased their U.S. Senate majority to fifty-five with a new class that will advocate common sense, conservative solutions to our big economic and social issues, and they picked up new seats in the U.S. House of Representatives. Republicans will now hold a record eighteen of the twenty-two U.S. Senate seats located in the eleven states of the "Old Confederacy." The margin of President Bush's victory, coupled with larger Republican congressional majorities, gives Republicans a clear opportunity to advocate and enact conservative, common sense solutions to our biggest issues.

Most political commentators predicted that the 2004 presidential election results would be as close as or closer than the results in 2000, and that again we would not have a decided president for months. Instead, voters turned out in record numbers across the nation to signal their intention that President Bush and the Republicans most represent their political values and ideologies. Why were Democratic candidates for federal office rebuked by the voters to such a degree, especially in an election that was supposed to be a referendum on the war on terror and a supposed weak economy?

Key National Election 2004 Voting Statistics

- Nationally, 11 percent of Blacks reported that they voted for President Bush, up from 9 percent in 2000.
- President Bush did better among Blacks in the "swing states" of Florida, Ohio, Pennsylvania, Wisconsin, and Minnesota, averaging from 12-16 percent support. President Bush had 18 percent support among Black voters in the Western Region of the U.S.
- 44 percent of Latinos reported that they voted for President Bush, up from 35 percent in 2000.
- 25 percent of Jewish voters supported President Bush, up from 19 percent in 2000.
- 52 percent of Catholic voters supported President Bush, up from 47 percent in 2000.
- 59 percent of Protestant voters supported President Bush, up from 56 percent in 2000.
- 22 percent of voters said they based their presidential vote on moral issues. 80 percent of these voters voted for President Bush.
- 11 states had initiatives on their ballots to ban same-sex marriage. The initiatives passed overwhelmingly in all 11.
- President Bush increased his margins of support among urban voters by 10 percentage points and among suburban voters by 3 percentage points.
- 34 percent of voters described themselves as ideologically "conservative," and 45 percent described themselves as "moderate." President Bush received 84 and 45 percent support, respectively, from these voter groups.

Two phenomena describe the modern Democratic Party and explain why it has lost touch with the mainstream U.S. electorate, why its candidates have lost the last two presidential elections, and why Republicans since the 1994 elections have kept control and gained seats in the U.S. House and Senate.

First, the Democratic Party is essentially a coalition of people who view themselves as members of a victimized or discriminated-against group, or as advocates for single liberal causes. This coalition includes pro-abortion, anti-war, and environmental activists, the majority of labor and teachers' union leaders, the majority of gays and lesbians, and many members of racial minorities. The coalition also includes liberal college professors, many members of the print, television, and radio media, and employees of various liberal think tank and policy research institutions. The coalition is held together by a shared belief in a more powerful, centralized federal government and an activist federal court system. As the results from the 2004 elections show, the issue positions and ideologies advocated by these radical groups and individuals do not represent the majority of political opinions in the U.S. Radical liberals try to position themselves as representative of the majority of the public, but their rhetoric does not match reality.

The second phenomenon that describes today's Democratic Party is that its support is based primarily on the West Coast, in the Northeast states, and in the urban areas of the nation's largest cities, including Atlanta, Detroit, Miami, and Chicago. The party that just a few years ago twice elected Bill Clinton as president, with 370 and 379 electoral votes respectively, has lost the ability to appeal to voters throughout the entire nation.

The results of the recent presidential, U.S. Senate, and U.S. House elections, shown in the following table, illustrate the regionalism phenomenon. The majority of U.S. Senate Democrats represent the nineteen states won by Senator Kerry, and the majority of U.S. House Democrats represent congressional districts in those states. Republicans clearly enjoy a broader

2004 Presidential, U.S. Senate, and U.S. House Election Comparison

Bush States Won	U.S. Senate Party Representation	U.S. House Party Representation
AK	2R	1R
AL	2R	5R, 2D
AR	2D	1R, 3D
AZ	2R	6R, 2D
CO	1R, 1D	4R, 3D
FL	1R, 1D	18R, 7D
GA	2R	7R, 6D
IA	1R, 1D	4R, 1D
ID	2R	2R
IN	1R,1D	7R, 2D
KS	2R	3R, 1D
KY	2R	5R, 1D
LA	1R, 1D	4R, 1D
MS	2R	2R, 2D
MO	2R	5R, 4D
MT	1R, 1D	1R
NC	2R	7R, 6D
ND	2D	1D
NE	1R, 1D	3R
NM	1R, 1D	2R, 1D
NV	1R, 1D	2R, 1D
OH	2R	12R, 6D
OK	2R	4R, 1D
SC	2R	4R, 2D
SD	1R, 1D	1D
TN	2R	4R, 5D
TX	2R	21R, 11D
UT	2R	2R, 1D
VA	2R	8R, 3D
WV	2D	1R, 2D
WY	2R	1R
TOTALS	**46R, 16D**	**146R, 76D**

Kerry States Won	U.S. Senate Party Representation	U.S. House Party Representation
CA	2D	20R, 33D
CT	2D	3R, 2D
DE	2D	1R
HI	2D	2D
IL	2D	9R, 10D
MA	2D	10D
MD	2D	2R, 6D
ME	2R	2D
MI	2D	9R, 6D
MN	1R, 1D	4R, 4D
NH	2R	2R
NJ	2D	6R, 7D
NY	2D	9R, 20D
OR	1R, 1D	1R, 4D
PA	2R	12R, 7D
RI	1R, 1D	2D
VT	1I, 1D	1I
WA	2D	3R, 6D
WI	2D	4R, 4D
TOTALS	9R, 28D, 1I	85R, 125D, 1I

range of support than Democrats. The majority of U.S. Senate Republicans represent the thirty-one states won by President Bush, and the majority of U.S. House Republicans represent congressional districts in the so-called red states (Republican).

The U.S. electorate seems to prefer strong leadership characteristics in their choice for president. The South in particular has preferred conservative presidents, in addition to men who exhibit strong leadership qualities. Ironically, two of our most liberal presidents, Jimmy Carter and Bill Clinton, were sons of the South and former Southern governors. So familiarity, coupled with regionalism, certainly played a role in their election and reelection campaigns, with the exception of the

1980 election of Ronald Reagan. Bill Clinton was viewed as a stronger leader in 1992 than incumbent George H. W. Bush and a stronger leader than his opponent for reelection, Kansas senator Robert Dole. Since 2000, the South has voted almost solidly Republican in elections for president and U.S. Senate. The Democrat senators who retired in 2004, such as Bob Graham in Florida, Ernest Hollings in South Carolina, John Edwards in North Carolina, and Zell Miller in Georgia, were all replaced by Republicans.

The election results of 2004 may signal the beginning of a period of dominance for the Republican Party at the federal level similar to the forty-year reign the Democrats had in Congress from 1955–1995 (see following table). But this dominance may not be realized if the Republican Party and its leaders do not do a better job of *reaching out* instead of expecting more people to *reach in.*

The reason for this shift toward increased public support of Republican candidates is that the federal courts and Congress, under control of the Democrats, took control of our biggest social and economic issues away from the individual states. Those issues that did belong under federal purview, such as the federal tax code and Social Security, were so abused and weakened by congressional Democrats that they are now completely beyond repair. The time to replace them is way past due!

The U.S. electorate has for now decided that the Republican Party better represents their social and economic values and ideologies than does the Democratic Party. The great irony in this situation is that Democrat-controlled House and Senate and liberal federal courts wrestled control of the big issues away from the individual states. For example, in 1973 the U.S. Supreme Court, led by a liberal, activist majority, decided in the famous *Roe v. Wade* case that women have a constitutional right to abort their unborn children. This ruling took away the power of states to make their own laws concerning abortion and made abortion-on-demand a federally-protected right.

Party Leadership at the Federal Level

Years	Majority in U.S. Senate	Majority in U.S. House	President's Party
1955-57	D	D	R
1957-59	D	D	R
1959-61	D	D	R
1961-63	**D**	**D**	**D**
1963-65	**D**	**D**	**D**
1965-67	**D**	**D**	**D**
1967-69	**D**	**D**	**D**
1969-71	D	D	R
1971-73	D	D	R
1973-75	D	D	R
1975-77	D	D	R
1977-79	**D**	**D**	**D**
1979-81	**D**	**D**	**D**
1981-83	R	D	R
1983-85	R	D	R
1985-87	D	D	R
1987-89	D	D	R
1989-91	D	D	R
1991-93	D	D	R
1993-95	**D**	**D**	**D**
1995-97	R	R	D
1997-99	R	R	D
1999-2001	R	R	D
2001-03	**R**	**R**	**R**
2003-05	**R**	**R**	**R**
2005-07	**R**	**R**	**R**

The federal tax code, enacted in 1913, and the Social Security system, enacted in 1935, essentially placed every citizen under the control and watchful eye of the federal government by mandating that a high percentage of the money we earn goes directly to the federal treasury to pay for entitlement programs and federal government spending we can no longer afford.

In 1980 Congress established the U.S. Department of Education, which took control of education policy and curriculums away from local school districts and the states and placed it in the hands of unaccountable bureaucrats in Washington, D.C. In 1977 Congress established the U.S. Department of Energy, which took control of decisions concerning development of new and efficient energy sources from the private sector. Because of this, private energy companies are now unable to explore domestic energy sources or build new nuclear power plants.

Finally, Democrats in control of Congress have sought to block the nomination of numerous federal judges proposed by Republican presidents whom they deem too conservative or who base their rulings too much on a strict reading of the Constitution. Instead, they have put in place judges from the Supreme Court on down who actively make law from the bench and who are unaccountable to the voters.

The old saying "If you live by the sword, you will die by the sword" is truly applicable to the reasons the Democrats have lost their tight grip of power in Washington, D.C. The liberal ideology advocated by the Democrat-controlled Congress, which believed in federal rather than state and local control of issues and policy, has failed the Democratic Party. Their arrogance and thirst for power blinded them to the fact that they could be voted out of office if they offended the electorate's common sense values and desire to place decision-making in the hands of local officials.

The liberal political ideology, whether exercised in the former Soviet Union, the current socialistic nations of Western Europe, or in the U.S. since the 1960s, mandates that citizens deny the existence of God, or at least advocate and tolerate the separation of God from secular society, and control of all major policy decisions at the federal level. The liberal ideology is propagated by a relatively few intellectual elites who share a mistrust that the general public is able to make their own decisions.

Liberal leaders fear most what they know in their hearts is true—that left to make their own decisions, voters in a free society will choose individual decision making at the local level, less federal government control of their lives, and let all who will listen know that God plays an important role in their lives. For most of the public, their inspiration comes from heaven, not from Washington, D.C. *Voters are not as dumb as Democrats think.*

Even though Democrats have been out of power in Congress for more than ten years, they still don't understand the public. The national Democratic leadership has abandoned any notion of centrist, moderate, or even conservative social and fiscal policies and is now solidly to the left of mainstream America's ideologies and values. In a story about the future of the Democratic Party following the 2004 congressional and presidential elections, Arizona governor Janet Napolitano, a Democrat, stated, "We need a fresh reassessment of how we communicate with people. How did a party that has been out of power in Washington, D.C., become tagged with the problems of Washington, D.C.? How did a party that is filled with people with values—and I am a person with values—get tagged as the party without values?" (Adam Nagourney, "Baffled in Loss, Democrats Seek Road Forward," *New York Times,* 7 November 2004).

Though she works in Arizona, Governor Napolitano suffers from the same "inside-the-beltway" thinking as her fellow party members in the U.S. House and Senate. The U.S. electorate "tagged her party" with the problems because these are problems that face the entire nation, not just the lawmakers in the U.S. Capitol. The war on terror, the approval of President Bush's judicial nominees, the possibility for federal court rulings in favor of same-sex marriage and partial-birth abortion, and our crumbling economic foundation are issues that affect our entire nation. The electorate chose the political party they thought has the best, common sense solutions to our problems, instead of the party that advocates solutions not supported by the mainstream. Governor Napolitano, you and your fellow party members may have values, but they are not the values shared by the majority of U.S. citizens.

Former U.S. Speaker of the House Tip O'Neill once famously stated that "All politics is local." In a sense, he was correct. People do not want the federal government to make their decisions for them and control their lives. Since control of the big issues now rests at the federal level, however, the electorate has decided that it supports the party that speaks to their values of individualism and personal responsibility. That party is not the Democrats.

Blacks and Conservative Democrats Have Been Taken for Granted

Since the early 1990s, Republicans have taken their common sense, conservative message to the former strongholds of the Democratic Party—the South, conservative Midwestern Democrats in the Plains and Rust Belt states, racial minorities, and young voters—as the Democrats' ideology embraced an increasingly liberal issue agenda that catered to the desires of its radical groups.

Instead of running toward the center, Democrats took their message to the ideological left in an attempt to keep what they thought was their traditional base of support. Again, the Democrats just don't get it. The majority of former Democratic support is not found in the fractured coalition of union leaders, gays and lesbians, proponents of big government, anti-war activists, pro-abortion activists, and those who wage class warfare. The Republicans cast a wider net than the Democrats in the 2004 elections and caught those in the ideological middle while not abandoning their conservative base.

At their core, members of groups that comprise the Democratic Party do not all share the same values. The elections of 2004 demonstrate that Democrats for years have abandoned their core constituency. Democratic leaders thought the groupthink mentality, forged for decades by the rhetoric of class and racial warfare, applied to all of their previous voters.

The voting patterns discussed above are primarily the voting patterns of Whites, who comprise the majority of the U.S. electorate. Since 1936, Blacks have voted at a rate of at least 60 percent for the Democratic candidate in presidential elections. Black Democrats are not in danger of being taken for granted by the White Democratic Party leaders or the self-appointed, so-called Black leaders. Their votes were taken for granted long ago. The question today is how long will Blacks allow themselves and their votes to be subject to the liberal ideology that dominates today's Democratic Party agenda?

Whites do not align themselves at a rate of nearly 90 percent with any particular party, and neither should Blacks. We do not have White issues, and we do not have Black issues. We have green issues—replacing the federal tax code, restructuring the Social Security system, and reducing the costs associated with the Medicare and health care systems. Whites align themselves with a political party and support candidates based on a sense of shared political ideology, but most Blacks choose to align themselves with one party based on tradition.

The Black electorate will cease to be taken for granted when a new generation of conservative Black leaders emerge who are legitimately and honestly motivated to advocate common sense policy solutions. The Democratic Party will then be forced to defend its liberal policy positions and solutions and explain why it has waited more than forty years to take action. At the same time, the Republican Party will have to continue to offer Black conservatives a seat at the table of policy development and aggressively campaign for the votes of the Black electorate.

What characteristics must the new Black political leaders possess? The first characteristic is *trust*. Black political leaders cannot be successful if they do not instill trust in the Black electorate that conservative policies will produce economic freedom and that the word "conservative" is not a synonym for "racist." If people feel they can trust you, both intellectually as well as emotionally, they will allow you to lead. Former congressman J. C. Watts wrote in his book *What Color Is a Conservative?* that "I really believe people want to know whether you share their concerns and values and what you intend to do to help solve their problems."

Instilling trust also requires scrapping the divisive rhetoric utilized for so many years by Democrats. The public demands real-world results, not the sound-bite rhetoric of Washington, D.C., and empty promises. They also demand a positive policy agenda and not more reasons why we should fear the other party.

The second characteristic new leaders must possess is *an ability to produce positive results.* Blacks will believe in the promise of conservative policy solutions when they see their personal economic situations improve, when schools improve and show dedication to educate every child, and when barriers are removed that prevent them from achieving their American Dreams.

The third characteristic demanded of new Black political leaders is *an ability to speak frankly* with people but to inspire them at the same time. A person's determination can be inspired to a higher level. Their belief in something can be inspired, their inner energy can be inspired, their faith can be inspired, and their motivation can be inspired. A leader's ability to inspire is determined most by the ability to communicate with words and symbolic actions. Words, phrases, and sentences delivered convincingly or with convincing passion inspire people. If done appropriately, actions can inspire as well as words. The most obvious action that can inspire occurs when the leader accomplishes what he or she determines to achieve or when the leader reaches a predetermined benchmark. An effective leader will then inspire people to set and achieve their own goals. As the late Morehouse College president Dr. Benjamin E. Mays used to tell us, "It must be borne in mind that the tragedy of life does not lie in not reaching your goals. The tragedy lies in not having any goals to reach for."

The Democratic Party has also taken the Hispanic electorate for granted. Increasing numbers of Hispanics are aware of that fact and have shown a willingness to support the Republican policy agenda. Hispanics represented 7 percent of the vote in the 2000 presidential election, and 62 percent voted for then vice president Al Gore. President Bush received 35 percent of the Hispanic vote in 2000. By 2004, Hispanics represented 8 percent of the vote, but President Bush increased his support among Hispanics by nine percentage points. Democratic candidate John Kerry received 53 percent of the Hispanic vote. Hispanics now slightly outnumber Blacks as a percentage of the U.S. population. As more and more Hispanic voters achieve economic success and begin to leave the Democratic plantation, they can expect to be subject to the same divisive and fear-based rhetoric currently targeted at conservative Black voters.

Though they have lost significant percentages of their traditional base, Democratic Party leaders still show an unwillingness to acknowledge that their radical liberal ideology does not match the values of the majority of U.S. citizens. U.S. House Minority Leader Nancy Pelosi, a California Democrat, admitted after election day in 2004 that "We were on a tough playing field." She went on to blame Democratic losses in key races on the fact that Republicans appealed more to socially and economically conservative former Democrats by emphasizing what she referred to as the "wedge issues" of same-sex marriage and abortion.

Is throwing more money at a broken Social Security system a wedge issue? No, it is simply stupid. Are raising taxes and taking more of peoples' hard-earned money to fund inefficient government programs wedge issues? No, it is insane, and people are sick and tired of it.

What Congresswoman Pelosi means by the term "wedge issues" is that these issues are simply distractions used by Republicans to drive a wedge between the Democratic Party and its former base. She does not think the electorate is intelligent enough to look at the entire policy agendas and issue positions of both parties and make a sound, informed decision. Democratic leaders still believe that the public only disagrees with them on one or two issues and agrees with them on most other issues. Wrong!

As my grandmother used to say, "Wishing doesn't make it so." People do not leave the political party they grew up with because of a disagreement over one issue. They leave when their party abandons its fundamental principles on the biggest issues and offers the wrong solutions to fix them. By labeling the biggest issues for many voters as wedge issues, the Democratic leaders show that they do not understand and therefore cannot address the biggest problems.

The fact that Democrats call such fundamental issues "wedge issues" demonstrates how out of touch they are with mainstream America. We live in a nation where most people have conservative social and economic values and where most people try to live their lives according to the morals and values taught to them in their church and by their parents. Most people do not think it is acceptable to abort unborn children or for people of the same sex to marry each other or to continue to waste taxpayers' money.

The majority of the public does not support removing the words "one nation under God" from our Pledge of Allegiance. They do not support removing the words "in God we trust" from our currency. They do not support presidents who carry on extra-martial affairs with interns in the Oval Office of the White House. Democrats simply cannot understand why most people involve their faith in making the big decisions in their lives. They cannot understand why people do not and cannot switch their faith on and off because of a notion of "separation between church and state"—a phrase that does not even appear in our Constitution! For most people, their religious faith, their personal and business lives, and their political views are inextricably intertwined.

For Democrats, "issue leadership" is a deceptive two-step process. First, they take a poll or conduct a focus group to determine what issues are most important to the public. Second, they frame the core liberal ideology and policy agenda around the issues most important to the public. The goal of this strategy is to fool the public into believing that the Democratic Party stands with the majority opinion on the electorate's core issues. They attempt to mimic the language and values of the public but in reality offer policies that are counter to the public's morals and values.

The Democratic Party's view of morality and the morality agenda they will offer the public in the coming congressional sessions and election years is not a morality based on biblical principles and traditional notions of right versus wrong taught by our parents and grandparents. Democrats will once again try to fool the public. They will argue that their traditional issue positions are more moral than the Republicans' positions. The Democrats, though, will not really side with the majority of people who know the difference between traditional and secular morality.

Instead, Democrats will argue that it is moral to pass an increase in the minimum wage. They will argue that that it is moral to enact a socialistic national health care system, paid for by the federal government, small businesses, and large corporations. They will argue that it is moral to tolerate the lifestyles of all citizens, no matter how aberrant we think they are. They will argue that tax increases are moral because tax increases indicate sacrifice and a sense of fairness. Democrats will not change their core beliefs and liberal ideology. They will only repackage their message and agenda and attempt to sell it to the public with a slick new marketing campaign.

Another example of Democratic Party leaders taking their base constituency for granted is when they advocate conservative policies in their home states but vote against these policies in Washington, D.C., where they think their voters are not paying attention. Throughout South Dakota Democrat and U.S. Senate Minority Leader Tom Daschle's 2004 reelection campaign, his opponent, Republican congressman John Thune, brought to light a number of examples of Daschle's long history of insincerity with South Dakota's voters. One example was Daschle's doublespeak on the issue of the global war on terrorism. Thune released a press statement that detailed Daschle's contradictory positions on the war:

> Senator Daschle's contradictory behavior is particularly noteworthy on the first anniversary of the beginning of the fall of Saddam Hussein and the liberation of Iraq. On the eve of military action beginning in Iraq, Senator Tom Daschle attacked President Bush: "I'm saddened, saddened that this president failed so miserably at diplomacy that we're now forced to war. Saddened that we have to give up one life because this president couldn't create the kind of diplomatic effort that was so critical for our country" (Senator Tom Daschle's remarks to AFSCME conference, 17 March 2003).
>
> Slightly less than a year later, after continuing to attack President Bush on Iraq, he suddenly reversed himself during a speech in South Dakota: "Senator Tom Daschle praised the Bush administration's war and nation-building work in Iraq and said he has no serious concerns about the lack of weapons of mass destruction. Daschle told state chamber of commerce representatives meeting in the South Dakota capital that he is satisfied with the way things are going in Iraq. He said he is not upset about the debate over pre-war intelligence on weapons of mass destruction, an issue that has dogged President Bush as Democratic presidential contenders have slogged through the primary season" (*Rapid City Journal*, 20 February 2004).

On election day, South Dakota's voters sent Minority Leader Daschle and the Democratic Party a message that voters are not fools and their votes could no longer be taken for granted when they voted him out of office and replaced him with the more conservative and trustworthy Congressman Thune.

Fortunately, the statistics from the 2004 elections show that some of the politically homeless are willing to leave the Democrat plantation and support conservative social and economic policies. The statistics show that Blacks, Hispanics, Jewish voters, and Catholic voters are no longer a monolith, bound by tradition and the rhetoric of their political leaders to vote for the Democratic candidate. These voters, who have found at least temporary shelter in the Republican Party, demonstrated by their votes that we can no longer view people simply as members of groups. Individuals from any race, ethnic background, or religious denomination have individual political ideologies and interests that transcend their skin color or church affiliation. Democrats will continue to view people as members of racial, religious, or victimized groups, treat them as such, and in doing so take them for granted, at their own peril.

Facts Don't Lie—Liars Ignore Facts

The biggest social and economic issues are blind to race. The current federal tax code is bad for everyone. The Social Security structure is bad for everyone, and the state of the Medicare system is bad for everyone. The rates of abortion, out-of-wedlock childbirths, and illiteracy directly or indirectly affect all members of society. If a significant percentage of our nation's youth are trapped in failing schools, unable and uninspired to learn, the negative repercussions will impact our economy and society for generations. The problems that adversely affect our economic and moral foundations have a negative impact on all citizens, but common sense solutions to our problems will benefit all citizens.

Though we all face the war waged on our economic and moral foundations, those at the lowest strata of economic achievement are the most adversely affected. The federal tax code has a negative impact on everyone, but it has a greater impact on the poor, which includes a disproportionate percentage of the racial minority population. The tax code was engineered in 1913 to raise money needed to fund wars, foreign and domestic programs, and the operations of federal government. In the almost one hundred years since it was enacted, it has ballooned to an eight-million-word mess that no one has ever completely read.

Over the years, Congress has added loopholes and tax credits that reward all manner of specific groups, organizations, and businesses. In doing so, Congress also created disincentives to individuals to start their own businesses, pursue the American entrepreneurial spirit, grow the economy, and pass their businesses and wealth on to their heirs. The federal tax code disproportionately hurts those from the lowest economic levels by increasing their tax burden as they make more money.

Every time the president or congressional Republicans discuss lowering the marginal tax rates by even one or two percentage points, eliminating whole brackets altogether, or replacing the tax code with a fairer system, Democrats in Congress and the liberal-dominated news media respond on cue that changes to the tax code will only benefit the rich. They do not even bother to check the facts or give people the facts. The amount of control the liberals can exercise over our lives is largely determined by how much of our money they can take from individuals and businesses in the form of taxes.

Federal government control over your life is exerted by redistributing to the poor, through an inefficient government program, the tax monies the government receives from you. In so doing, the government controls you by limiting the amount of money you have to spend, save, and invest. The government also controls the recipient of its largess because if poor people or other government dependents improve themselves financially, they are no longer eligible to receive government assistance. Over time, the recipients often lose incentive to better their lives and get off the government dole.

At the same time, middle to upper class income earners who had their income taxed lose incentive to create more wealth through investments or grow businesses because their increased earnings could easily push them into an even higher marginal tax bracket. Only the very wealthy can take advantage of the special tax loopholes written into the tax code, such as making enough money from the dividends of tax-free municipal bonds or setting up corporations and paying themselves as employees.

Liberal congressional Democrats actually attempt to convince the public that this is a fair system that benefits everyone but the rich. In reality, no one benefits from the federal tax code except liberals in Congress who feel they are smarter and better equipped than you to make the decisions that most affect your life. Unfortunately, liberals have been somewhat successful in maintaining their control through manipulation of the tax code. They have instilled in millions of U.S. citizens a sense of jealousy and class envy against those in the highest income brackets. They have created a mentality among the poor and those not educated in elementary economics, those who do not pay a significant percentage of income taxes anyway, that the best and fairest way to fund the activities of government is to punish those who work hard and achieve economic success. Instead of eliminating barriers so that all citizens have the opportunity to achieve, liberals seek to create more barriers to achievement and increase the number of people dependent upon their programs.

Democrats do not want the public to study history or become versed in the dynamics of elementary economics. When President Reagan took office in 1981, the top marginal tax rate was 50 percent. He cut that rate to 28 percent, which provided the impetus for the historic economic growth that occurred in the 1980s and 1990s. President Kennedy introduced a plan in 1963 to lower the highest marginal tax rate of 91 percent to 70 percent, which sparked similar economic growth. Democrats are not happy when Republicans laud President Kennedy's tax-cutting measures. They seem to be embarrassed that "one of their own" committed the sin of tax rate reduction.

The fact is, replacing the federal tax code will benefit all citizens and provide people from all income brackets with incentives to create wealth, save more money, and invest more

How Progressive Is the FairTax?

A federal retail sales tax on new goods and services that replaces all income and payroll taxes

Effective tax rates	Current system	FairTax system
Single parent / two children / minimum wage Annual income: $10,712 / year	3.3%	-2.9%
A couple living solely on Social Security Annual income: $25,944 / year	22.0%	10.3%
Married couple / two children Annual income: $32,136	31.5%	9.2%
Single mother / two children and mortgage Annual income: $45,000	30.2%	10.6%
Married couple / two children and mortgage Annual income: $65,000	30.5%	13.6%
Married couple / two children / homeowner Annual income: $100,000	33.8%	15.0%

money in their futures and the futures of their children and grandchildren. In the 1990s I became chairman of the Tax Leadership Council for an organization called Americans for Fair Taxation (AFFT). AFFT is the organization responsible for promoting replacement of the current federal tax code with a national retail sales tax, also known as the FairTax.

The idea of replacing the federal income tax with the FairTax is gaining grassroots support and momentum across the country. It was introduced in Congress by Georgia congressman John Linder and in the Senate by Georgia senator Saxby Chambliss. The FairTax legislation has more than fifty co-sponsors. The FairTax will replace the current federal tax code with a national retail sales tax on all new goods and services. Replacement of the federal tax code with the FairTax will result in an immediate increase in take-home pay for all wage earners and effectively "untax" the poor (see table on previous page). You can read more about the benefits of the FairTax at www.fairtax.org.

The Social Security structure is broken beyond repair, but Congress has never shown the political will necessary to fix it. The Social Security system will be unable to meet the demands of the baby-boomer retirees and, left in its current condition, will be fiscally insolvent before most of the baby boomers die. Subsequent generations can expect to receive zero return on their lifetime of contributions to the system.

A number of solutions have been offered to save Social Security, including President Bush's proposal to enact an optional system of personal retirement accounts. Instead of working on a solution to the looming Social Security crisis, however, Congress continues to shirk its responsibilities to the public by increasing the retirement age and decreasing benefits to future retirees.

The current Social Security structure adversely affects all citizens, but it has the greatest negative effect on racial minorities. For example, due to the disparity in average life expectancy for Black men—sixty-eight years versus seventy-five years for White males—Blacks can expect on average only a few years of low benefits from the Social Security system. If Congress continues to increase each year the retirement age to receive benefits, Blacks and others with lower average life expectancies could find themselves contributing all their lives to a system but virtually guaranteed to receive zero return on their investment.

The current Social Security structure also has a disproportionately adverse affect on the poor and those below the median income level, regardless of race, due to the increasing income limit used to determine who automatically pays Social Security taxes. The highly regressive Social Security payroll tax only taxes wages, the primary or singular source of income for most of the poor. Workers making more than $90,000 do not pay payroll taxes on their income over that limit. The entire salaries of workers making less than the limit are therefore subject to the Social Security payroll tax. If Congress raises the amount subject to payroll taxation, the salaries of millions of workers will forever be reduced to pay for the failed Social Security system.

Liberals do not want to face the reality that the Social Security structure is insolvent. Congressional liberals view the Social Security system as a mechanism to fund all their favorite social engineering programs, since the payroll taxes contributed to the system go straight to Congress's general fund. The Social Security payroll tax is another mechanism designed to relieve you of your money and provide you nothing in return. Millions of citizens should question why we keep in place a retirement system that is not funded at the necessary levels to meet the demand of the coming baby-boomer retirees, will require increasingly high and regressive payroll tax increases to sustain, and provides a zero percent return on your investment—if you live long enough to receive all the money you paid in.

To liberal Democrats, the nation's economy is never prosperous when Republicans control the presidency, Congress, or both, and it is only getting worse. According to Democratic candidates and most media sources during the 2004 election cycle, the U.S. economy was stagnant, struggling, and losing jobs. They argued that President Bush was responsible for an economy that produced more than two million job losses since his election. The Democrats and their accomplices in the media neglected, of course, to mention the reasons jobs were lost at the beginning of the first Bush administration—the "dot-com" burst of the late 1990s, numerous corporate scandals, and the terrorist attacks on New York City's World Trade Center on September 11, 2001.

In reality, the 2004 economy showed declining unemployment, increases in jobs in many sectors, and strong economic growth as measured by higher hourly earnings, increases in home purchases and construction, and increases in Gross Domestic Product. Media stories about job creation and unemployment have not been consistent. In 1996 during President Clinton's reelection campaign, stories were positive 85 percent of the time—more than four times as often as they were for President Bush—even though the unemployment rate measured at the same times of the year was lower in 2004 and the economy added two million jobs from 2003 to 2004 alone.

Comparison of the Metrics on U.S. Economy, 1996 and 2004

Economic Indicator	Clinton 1996	Bush 2004
Unemployment	5.2%	5.4%
Gross Domestic Product Growth	2.2%	4.5%
Inflation	3.0%	2.7%
Continuous Months of Positive Job Growth	7	12

Source: Media Research Center's Free Market Project

Moreover, the Joint Center for Political and Economic Studies found in its *2004 National Opinion Poll* that 60 percent of Blacks surveyed, and 70 percent overall, considered themselves financially the same or better off than in the previous year.

A key component to the Democrat policy agenda since the Clinton administration of the 1990s has been to enact a nationalized health care system that covers all the health care costs of all U.S. citizens. A nationalized health care system would destroy the free-market incentives to improve health care and develop new and better pharmaceutical drugs, and the quality and accessibility to health care services would plummet.

In 1994, as vice chairman of the National Restaurant Association, I was part of a nationwide initiative to help raise awareness that the Clinton Health Care Plan was an economic and social disaster. President Clinton stated on numerous occasions that the cost of his health care plan for service businesses like restaurants would only be about 2.5 percent of the cost of doing business and that he did not understand why the restaurant industry's opposition was so intense. My staff and I had been through the calculations many times, and we continued to find that for many restaurant businesses, the president's calculations were way off!

I was asked at that time to participate in a live town hall meeting the president would conduct in Kansas City, with hookups to audiences in Omaha, Nebraska; Tulsa, Oklahoma; and Topeka, Kansas. I jumped at the opportunity to address President Clinton about his health care plan and the fact that his administration had miscalculated its true cost.

I attended the April 1994 town hall meeting at a television studio in Omaha. When the second round of questions began, I was informed that I would be the next to ask President Clinton a question. I have to admit this was one of the few times in my life that I truly felt a little nervous. It was not nervousness because of Bill Clinton but because of my respect for the office of president of the United States of America, the highest office of the greatest nation on the face of the earth.

My turn soon came, and I rose to speak. Our conversation went as follows:

> Herman Cain (HC): "Mister President, thank you very much for this opportunity, and I would like to commend you on making health care a national priority. [*The president nodded politely.*] In your State of the Union speech, you indicated that nine out of ten Americans currently have health care insurance, primarily through their employers. And tonight you indicated that out of those people who do not have insurance, eight out of ten of them work for someone. And your plan would force employers to pay this insurance for those people that they currently do not cover. I would contend that employers who do not cover employees do not for one simple reason, and it relates to cost."

Next, I explained I had calculated what his program would cost Godfather's Pizza, Inc., and that I had also spoken with hundreds of other business people about his program's impact on their operations.

> HC: "The cost of your plan is simply a cost that will cause us to eliminate jobs. In going through my own calculations, the number of jobs that we would have to eliminate to try to absorb this cost is a lot greater than I ever anticipated. Your averages about the impact on smaller businesses—those are all well intended—but all of the averages represent a wide spectrum in terms of the businesses impacted. On behalf of all of those business owners that are in a similar situation to mine, my question is, quite simply, if I'm forced to do this, what will I tell those people whose jobs I will have to eliminate?"

Instead of answering my question, the president proceeded to try to convince me and the audience that the impact of his plan on my business (and therefore, on other restaurants and small businesses) would be minimal.

President Clinton: "So suppose you have part-time workers and some wouldn't have to be covered. So you wouldn't go from two and one-half percent of payroll to seven point nine percent. You might go to something like six percent. If you had six percent of payroll . . . let's just say six and one-half percent, that's a good, even number. You had four percent of payroll—and that's one-third of your total cost. So you would add about one and a half percent to the total cost of doing business. Would that really cause you to lay a lot of people off? If all your competitors have to do it, too? Only if people stopped eating out. If all your competitors had to do it and your cost of doing business went up one and a half percent . . . wouldn't that leave you in the same position you are in now? Why wouldn't they all be in the same position? And why wouldn't you all be able to raise the price of pizza two percent? I'm a satisfied customer. I'd keep buying from you."

Not only was President Clinton's arithmetic incorrect, but it didn't even make sense! His suggestion that all of my competitors would also raise their prices amounted to illegal price fixing, even if the government effectively mandated the price increase, and it shows a severe lack of understanding of Economics 101. Even if the president's proposal were possible, to pass along a 7.9 percent increase would require about a 16 percent price increase on the products my company sold.

HC: "Okay. First of all, Mr. President, with all due
respect, your calculation on what the impact would
do, quite honestly, is incorrect."

I then proceeded to explain to the president the errors in his
calculations and the difficulties associated with recovering
profits by simply raising prices. President Clinton got the last
word in our exchange:

President Clinton: "Let me ask you a favor. Would
you send to me, personally, your calculations because
I know we've got to go on to other questions."

I did send the president my calculations in a letter that appeared
in the *Wall Street Journal*, the *Omaha World Herald*, and several
other newspapers. And the response I received from the head of
the Small Business Administration, Erskine Bowles, did not
challenge my calculations, logic, or rationale. Instead, his
response attempted to rationalize how much better off society
in general would be under the president's plan, regardless of its
impact on business or the economy. That was the last I heard
from the president or his administration. They simply chose to
ignore the facts.

Specifically, I felt that the Clinton Health Care Plan was a
job killer, a bureaucracy builder, and a non-solution to the
wrong problem. The president had even acknowledged in his
State of the Union address that approximately nine out of ten
people were already covered with health insurance. So why not
look for effective ways of providing access for the remaining 10
percent while allowing market forces to bring the cost of health
care down? As I told NBC news anchor Tom Brokaw during a
network television health care special, "If I have a leak in the
roof and I know that the roof is leaking, I don't blow up the
building to fix the leak in the roof."

In September 1994, I was informed by Oregon senator Bob
Packwood, one of the leading Republican senators opposing the
president's proposal, that Senate Democrats had finally given up
on passing the Clinton Health Care Plan. More than ten years
later, Democratic leaders are still advocating a plan to enact a
nationalized health care system. Liberal Democrats have shown
through the years that they will not let a little adversity or a few
setbacks stop them from enacting their favorite policies.
Conservatives must stay as vigilant in fighting their ill-conceived
plans while educating the public about common sense solutions
to the right problems.

One common sense solution signed into law by President
Bush in December 2003 is the establishment of Health Savings
Accounts. These accounts allow untaxed dollars to be used to
buy health insurance and to pay medical expenses. More
importantly, these accounts allow people to take ownership of
their health insurance away from government.

The issue of same-sex marriage was a hot issue in the 2004
session of the Georgia legislature and across the nation. Eleven
states featured ballot initiatives on election day that asked voters
if they support a ban on legalizing same-sex unions. The initiatives passed overwhelmingly in all eleven states. Rev. Cameron
Alexander, my pastor at Antioch Baptist Church in Atlanta, had
a reply ready to those in his congregation who asked him his
position on the same-sex marriage issue: "What part of the Bible
do you want to throw out?"

If you believe in the Bible, then the issue is a moot point. We
cannot separate this "civil rights issue," as the Democrats call it,
from the moral issue. There is a tendency among liberals to
lower a moral standard to accommodate a civil behavior. If we
had done that with "All men are created equal," Black people
would still be in slavery.

The difference between the civil rights struggle and the so-
called gay rights struggle is that the civil rights struggle
constantly moved this nation upward to live up to the ideal that

"All men are created equal, endowed by their Creator." The gay rights struggle involves altering the established moral principle of marriage as the union between one man and one woman. If you begin with the moral principle that marriage is between one man and one woman, they are asking the nation to alter their moral principles to accommodate a civil behavior. When society lowers its moral ideals, it goes adrift, and it will drift into oblivion. Liberal advocates of gay marriage attempted to frame the argument in favor of their position around the civil rights struggle of the 1950s and 1960s. Voters of all races and demographic backgrounds were not fooled. When people learn the facts about social issues like abortion and same-sex marriage and the negative impact they have on our nation, the Democrats lose more support for their radical agendas.

Many of the Politically Homeless Have Already Left the Plantation

Most people are not totally partisan in the sense that they only support candidates with a (D) or (R) after their names. Voters in some of the states that supported President Bush also voted for a Democratic candidate for Senate. Republican senators represent some states from the traditionally liberal Northeast. Many Republican and Democrat members of the U.S. House who hold political views across the ideological spectrum represent voters who reward their records, not their party labels.

Significant shifts in party balance at the federal level occur when senators and representatives abandon their constituencies' core values. Republicans gained four more seats in the U.S. Senate in 2004 because voters in their respective states lost trust in the Democratic leadership's ability to support mainstream values.

The Democratic Party and its surrogates launched a campaign of hate against President Bush immediately following the 2000 presidential election, yet support for the president in

2004 increased among nearly every voter demographic. Liberal media outlets, Democratic Party leaders and elected officials, Hollywood actors, musicians, writers, and columnists waged a four-year war of negative, divisive propaganda against President Bush unlike any political rhetoric we have ever seen. The more the Democrat establishment turned up the volume on their own ideas, however, the more they drove conservative voters to the polls in support of the president.

The politically homeless were energized in 2004 by their opportunity to have a voice in national policymaking decisions. Some supported Republican candidates and others supported Democrats, but they were inspired by their choices and took advantage of their opportunity to select new leadership.

Evangelical Christians are more politically active because the social issues are coming under increasing control of the courts and federal and state governments. Twenty-three percent of voters in 2004 identified themselves as White and born-again or evangelical Christians. Seventy-eight percent of these voters supported President Bush's conservative social agenda. Conservative Black, Hispanic, Jewish, and Catholic voters similarly joined the ranks of those who see the liberal Democratic social policy agenda as an attack on our nation's moral foundations.

Increasing numbers of the politically homeless from all demographics are leaving their ancestral home on the Democratic plantation. They are gradually waking up to the issues and the facts and becoming less responsive to the divisive, hollow rhetoric of the radical liberals in the Democratic Party. The process of letting go of past party affiliations, however, is slow. It will require both trustworthy leadership from national Republican Party leaders and politicians and a concerted grassroots movement across the country, driven by inspired individuals with a passion for change. The politically homeless, active at the grassroots level of political involvement, can close the great divides and force Congress and the president to be more honest and accountable to the citizens they represent.

After my town hall meeting chat with President Clinton, many people wrote to me or called expressing how happy they were to see me asking the president the right question and informing him of the errors in his calculations. Many people went on to comment that they were now inspired to write or call their own senators or representatives because they shared my views about the negative impact of his health care plan on jobs. I never expected one event to inspire so many people to speak up and to speak out.

The politically homeless spoke up and spoke out and found a temporary home in the Republican Party in the 2004 elections. Why? Many voters are just not as dumb as Democrats think, and they are a lot smarter than Republicans think. But can the Republicans keep them?

Voters Are Not as Dumb as Democrats Think

History Is Not on the Democrats' Side

- Even though Democrats claim to be the party that champions civil rights, history and the facts are not on their side. In every case, Democrats fought the hardest to deny the civil rights of the voters they now take for granted. History is clearly on the side of Republicans relative to civil rights legislation.

- The Democratic Party is losing more and more voters because it has become a coalition of people who view themselves as members of a victimized or discriminated-against group or as single-issue advocates for liberal causes. Many of the politically homeless found temporary shelter in the Republican Party on election day in 2004 when they cast their votes in support of the conservative policy agenda.

- People do not want the federal government to make their decisions for them and control their lives. The electorate has decided that it supports the party that speaks to their values of individualism and personal responsibility. But if the Republicans do not deliver, they will quickly return to minority party status.

Blacks and Conservative Democrats Have Been Taken for Granted

- Instead of moving toward the center, Democrats took their message to the ideological left in an attempt to keep what they thought was their traditional base of support. People do not leave the political party with which they grew up because of a disagreement over one relatively minor issue. They leave when their party abandons its fundamental principles on the biggest issues and when their party offers the wrong solutions to fix them.

- The Black electorate has been taken for granted with divisive rhetoric and empty promises instead of common sense policy solutions.
- Democratic Party leaders have taken their base constituency for granted by advocating conservative policies in their home states while voting against these policies in Washington, D.C., where they think their voters are not paying attention.

Facts Don't Lie—Liars Ignore Facts

- The biggest social and economic issues are blind to race. The current federal tax code is bad for everyone. The Social Security structure is bad for everyone, and the state of the Medicare system is bad for everyone. They all have a greater impact on racial minorities and the poor.
- Presidents Kennedy, Reagan, and now George W. Bush were able to reduce taxes. In each case the actions stimulated the economy. Democrats keep telling people tax cuts don't work and that they only benefit the rich. They choose to ignore the facts!
- Replacement of the federal tax code with the FairTax would lower the total taxes paid by everybody. It would also produce the same amount of revenue by expanding the tax base.

Many of the Politically Homeless Have Already Left the Plantation

- Significant shifts in party balance at the federal level occur when senators and representatives abandon their constituencies' core values. Increasing numbers of the politically homeless are gradually waking up to the issues and the facts and becoming less responsive to the divisive,

hollow rhetoric of the radical liberals in the Democratic
Party.

- The active politically homeless at the grassroots level of
political involvement can close the great divides and force
Congress and the president to be more accountable to the
citizens they represent.

Chapter 4

Voters Are Smarter Than Republicans Think

The Republican Party won big on Election Day in 2004 by recapturing the White House and adding to its majorities in both the U.S. House and Senate. In addition, a majority of states have Republican governors, including the four largest states of California, Florida, New York, and Texas. Given the current majority status Republicans enjoy across the nation, though, the electorate is far from unified behind any one political party or political ideology. Many of the politically homeless found a temporary home in the Republican Party in 2004, but Republicans still cannot convince many of these temporary residents to identify themselves as Republicans. This also means that there is no guarantee of future support.

We can see from the following table that an equal percentage of voters (37%) identify themselves as Democrat or Republican, but that more voters (45%) consider themselves ideologically moderate, as opposed to liberal or conservative.

2004 Presidential Election: Self-identified Party I.D. and Political Ideology

Party Identification	Percent of Voters	Voted for Bush (2004)	Voted for Bush (2000)	Voted for Kerry
Democrat	37%	11%	11%	89%
Republican	37%	93%	91%	6%
Independent	26%	48%	47%	49%
Political Ideology				
Liberal	21%	13%	13%	85%
Moderate	45%	45%	44%	54%
Conservative	34%	84%	81%	15%

Source: CNN.com 2004 Presidential Election Exit Poll

Democratic presidential candidate John Kerry fared nine percentage points better than Republican president George W. Bush among the self-identified moderate voters, and each candidate captured double-digit support from voters who are presumably on the opposite end of the ideological spectrum from their respective policy agendas. As we have seen in every presidential election since 1992, the 2004 outcome was far from a landslide victory for the winning candidate.

The following table illustrates the issues most important to voters in the 2004 presidential election, and for which candidate voters cast their ballot based on the issue most important to them.

2004 Presidential Election: Voters' Most Important Issue

Most Important Issue	Percent of Voters	Voted for Bush	Voted for Kerry
Taxes	5%	57%	43%
Education	4%	26%	73%
Iraq	15%	26%	73%
Terrorism	19%	86%	14%
Economy/Jobs	20%	18%	80%
Moral Values	22%	80%	18%
Health Care	8%	23%	77%

Source: CNN.com 2004 Presidential Election Exit Poll

We can see in the above table that the top three issues for voters in 2004 were moral values, the status of the economy and job growth, and the global war on terrorism. Of these three issues, President Bush received overwhelming support from those who view moral values and the war on terrorism as most important. Senator Kerry received the vast majority of support from voters who viewed the economy as the most important issue, which is consistent with his persistent rhetoric throughout his campaign. President Bush's campaign was clearly able to frame the election as a referendum on his leadership in winning the war on terrorism, while capitalizing on the majority of the public's opposition to legalizing same-sex marriage as a major moral issue.

What is perhaps most telling about the data in the above table is that, when given the opportunity, voters viewed the war on terrorism and U.S. military action against terrorists in Iraq as two separate issues. Voters were clearly more supportive of President Bush's overall handling of the war on terrorism than on the status of the war in Iraq. Voters also saw the status of the economy as an issue separate from how each candidate would deal with the issue of taxation.

The disconnect in voters' minds between the war on terrorism and the war in Iraq and the relationship between the status of the economy and the effect of taxes on the economy demonstrate that the Bush administration and Republican congressional leaders have done a poor job in communicating to the electorate the undeniable connections between these issues. Although the positive economic indicators were compelling during most of 2004 versus the indicators during President Clinton's reelection year of 1996, Republicans were only mildly successful at countering the negative campaign rhetoric from Democrats and liberal media outlets.

While sitting in as substitute host for Martha Zoller's popular radio talk show, I spoke with a listener who called and said there was no way he would vote for President Bush because of the terrible state of the economy. When I asked him on what facts he had based his assessment as terrible, he responded that he had no facts. He had truly drunk every drop of the Democratic Kool-Aid.

The following table illustrates how members of various racial backgrounds voted in the 2004 presidential election. President Bush increased his percentage of support among voters in all racial backgrounds from 2000 to 2004, but he still received less than 45 percent support from all groups except Whites. In addition, Bush's support among Black voters fell short of expectations. In a poll conducted prior to the election by the Joint Center for Political and Economic Studies, 18 percent of Blacks overall indicated they would vote for President

2004 Presidential Election: Vote by Race

Vote by Race	Percent of Voters	Voted for Bush (2004)	Voted for Bush (2000)	Voted for Kerry
White	77%	58%	54%	41%
African-American	11%	11%	9%	88%
Latino	8%	44%	35%	53%
Asian	2%	44%	41%	56%

Source: CNN.com 2004 Presidential Election Exit Poll

Bush, which included 36 percent support among self-identified conservative Christian Blacks.

The polling results detailed in the above tables show that the politically homeless who took shelter in the Republican Party in 2004 were primarily White conservative voters who were energized to vote because they wanted to maintain our current leadership during war and also by the necessity to defend our nation from attacks on our moral foundations. The majority of Black, Latino, Asian, and ideologically moderate voters have still not been persuaded by the Republican Party to embrace the Republican policy agenda.

Further, many conservative Republicans were frustrated by policies enacted or advocated in President Bush's first term, particularly massive federal spending on new entitlement programs and proposals to stem the flow of illegal aliens across our borders. They were not frustrated enough to vote against President Bush, but they were still unhappy at times.

One initiative that upset many conservative supporters of President Bush was the Medicare Prescription Drug Improvement and Modernization Act of 2003. Beginning in January 2006, all forty million Medicare patients, regardless of financial need, will be allowed to sign up for a benefit that provides reductions in the cost of their prescription medications. The cost estimates for this new Medicare entitlement top five hundred billion dollars and will surely exceed that figure throughout the life of the program. Just look at the history of the growth in Medicare costs.

In 1965, when Medicare was first enacted, it cost six billion dollars to implement. The estimated cost twenty-five years into the program (1990) was supposed to be twelve billion dollars. The actual cost in 1990 was 109 billion dollars! That's a 900 percent miss! For most conservatives, this new Medicare entitlement is directly opposite to the conservative ideology of restrained federal spending and responsible budgeting.

President Bush also upset many conservatives with his plan to allow illegal aliens to legally hold jobs in the U.S. The plan would make illegal aliens eligible for temporary legal status for six years, as long as they are employed. Presumably, they could reapply after six years. The plan would not, however, allow them to automatically become citizens at the end of any six-year period. President Bush argued that this new program would allow illegal workers who currently hold jobs to come out of hiding and participate legally in the U.S. economy, while not encouraging further illegal behavior.

Although President Bush should be commended for trying to fix a problem he inherited from decades of Congress not dealing with the issue, conservative Republicans viewed that proposal as a "shadow citizenship" plan for people who came to this country illegally. And unlike what the administration believes, conservatives believe such a plan would encourage further illegal behavior and that it amounts to granting amnesty to those here illegally.

U.S. House Majority Leader Tom Delay, a Texas Republican, stated that he has "heartfelt reservations about allowing illegal immigrants into a U.S. guest-worker program that seems to reward illegal behavior" (Ralph Z. Hallow, "GOP to finesse immigration issue," *The Washington Times*, 23 August 2004). Many other Republican politicians shared Delay's concerns, and Bush's proposal prompted citizens across the country to mobilize in opposition and voice their objections to what they feel is the wrong solution to a grave and growing problem.

Congressional Republicans since 1994, as well as the Bush administration since 2000, have demonstrated leadership in dealing with our enemies abroad and have achieved a number of legislative victories in domestic policy, such as tax cuts, reforms in public education, and welfare reform. Unfortunately, the Republican Party and its candidates continue to suffer defeats in the public relations arena because they do not adequately connect the rationale behind their policy agendas in a language that relates to the political layperson.

The Bush administration allowed Democrats and members of liberal media outlets to separate the war on terrorism from many of the reasons the U.S. went to war against Iraqi leaders. Iraqi leaders were, in fact, sponsoring global terrorist activities and murdering millions of their own citizens. Democrats framed the war in Iraq as a search for weapons of mass destruction. When no large caches of such weapons were found, Democrats and their accomplices in the media accused Bush and the Republicans of losing the war on terrorism, making the U.S. unsafe, and prosecuting the war in Iraq to increase oil companies' profits.

Republicans have also done a poor job communicating the effects of cutting or eliminating income, dividend, and estate tax rates on producing economic growth, job creation, and individual prosperity. They mistakenly assume that most of the public understands elementary economics. They do not. Instead of framing the issue of tax cuts around the personal benefits available to individual taxpayers, such as more money in their pockets, and their companies will be less likely to lay people off from their jobs, Republicans defend tax rate reductions by arguing that federal coffers will swell and businesses will grow and hire more employees. Individuals care more about not being laid off than they do about a business growing.

While the Republicans are technically correct, Republicans must remember that businesses do not vote in elections. Leroy and Bessie Public vote in elections, and in the back of their minds is the thought that the Democrats might be right when they charge that tax cuts only benefit the rich.

The Republican Party demonstrated in 2004 that it is capable of turning out large numbers of voters who support a conservative policy agenda. It failed, however, in getting many of the politically homeless to feel comfortably at home as full-fledged Republicans.

To borrow a term popular in business and marketing, the Republican Party has a "brand identity problem" that it has not solved for many voters. You can have the best product, but if it is not perceived as the best product, you lose. If the Republicans solve their brand identity problem, they have the opportunity to persuade many of the politically homeless that their long-term economic interests, and the best interests of the entire nation, rest with the Republican agenda to protect our economic and moral foundations. The conversion will not be a revolution. But it can be a rapid evolution.

Republicans Have a Brand Identity Problem

The Democratic Party has successfully convinced millions of Americans—primarily those in their favorite groups—that Republicans represent only the interests of wealthy Whites and Fortune 500 companies. Democrats accomplished this task by instilling in their members powerful feelings of jealousy rooted in a haves vs. have-nots mentality and by blaming Republicans for creating great disparities among the public in wealth and economic achievement.

Republicans have attempted to counter the Democrats' false claims and logically challenged ideology, but it takes generations to undo political beliefs more than seventy years in the making. Many of the politically homeless are not ready to support Republican candidates because Republicans have not made serious attempts to connect to voters in the traditional Democratic base and explain why their policy positions and solutions to the big issues benefit all citizens, regardless of race, religion, or economic background.

Whereas the Democratic Party has an *ideology problem*, the Republican Party has a *brand identity problem*. Brand identity is based upon people's perceptions of you and your message. Brand identity for a product, a business, or a political party is driven by one thing—messages in the mind over time. Those messages create brand identity, over time, in the mind of the consumer.

My business goggles taught me that people hear not just with their ears, but they hear with their hearts, their eyes, and their heads. The ears are simply a vehicle to feed the heart, the eyes, and the head. Democrats usually go right for the heart with emotional rhetoric. Republicans usually go to the head with facts and an understanding of the logic.

When I became CEO of Godfather's Pizza in 1986, it was a failing company. The company literally was about to go under. Our sales were declining, company morale was declining, and our brand identity was blurred. My own management team and employees no longer knew the Godfather's mission. My number one task was to get everyone to realize that we had a brand identity crisis. Our management team had forgotten, and our customer base had forgotten, that Godfather's made the best-tasting pizza. Why? Because we gradually stopped making the best-tasting pizza. As a result, we lost customers, we lost profitability, and we were losing our company.

Both political parties spend millions of dollars trying to sell their brand identity during elections, when a lot of the perception of their brand is created between elections by . . . (*drum roll*) the media.

Let's illustrate the power of brand identity. If I were to say the term "Big Blue," what company pops into your mind? How long did it take you to answer IBM? If I were to say "copiers," what product comes to mind? Most likely, it is Xerox. How many times have you done as I have done and incorrectly said, "Would you make a Xerox of this for me?" Or "I'd like a Coke," and someone brings you another cola product. These are examples of strong brand identity. The brand is so strong that it becomes synonymous with the product.

Strong messages are not enough, though, to create a strong, positive brand identity. The messages must be credible. There must be substance underlying the message. At Godfather's we decided to have one goal—make the best-tasting pizza. To achieve this goal we had to eliminate a lot of barriers that prevented us from achieving this goal. It's called focus. Basically, Godfather's was trying to be all things to all people before I arrived. They were trying to provide multiple products to multiple groups of consumers in an attempt to attract everybody. Instead of achieving "the best-tasting pizza," they ended up with a conglomeration of poor products.

This is the direction the Democrats have taken their political party, and the Republicans have started to drift in that direction by losing their focus on fiscal responsibility. The Democrats tell anyone who will listen that their policies appeal to that person or their group and that the competition (the Republican Party) is too busy focusing on one consumer group (the rich) to care about them.

When most people stop and really look at the primary tenets of what it means to be a Republican, they quickly realize that they are more ideologically aligned with the Republican Party. But they quickly go back to their perception of the party and denounce any formal affiliation. That's the weakness of the brand.

The Republican Party has allowed its primary competition (Democrats) to define its image and what it stands for. Because of this, there now exists among millions of citizens a perception of what a Republican is that differs from the reality of what it means to be a Republican.

Do you remember the story about Scotty, the college sophomore who accompanied me one day as part of a job shadow project at his school? Scotty told me, "A Democrat stands for the little people and a Republican stands for the rich guy."

I then asked Scotty if he had heard of the term "GOP."

He said, "Yes."

I said, "Do you know what GOP means?"

Scotty replied, "No."

I said, "What if I told you it stood for 'Grand Old Party'? What would that suggest to you?"

"Sounds like a bunch of old dudes," Scotty answered.

Perception has been allowed to cloud reality. The Republican brand is perceived by many Democrats as showing a lack of compassion toward the poor, the elderly, and children in public schools. The brand is thought by millions to be unaccepting of racial minorities and uncaring about blue-collar workers struggling to achieve their American Dreams. Nothing is further from the truth, but a lot people do not know it. As a result, Republicans are experiencing difficulty connecting to the all-important middle or *politically homeless* voter.

How did the Republicans allow themselves to become perceived as an uncaring, unaccepting, uncompassionate party comprised of "old dudes"? For too many years, Republicans have done little to combat the negative and divisive rhetoric of the Democrats and liberal members of the print and television media. In addition, Republicans do not package their message in a format that connects on a personal level with Leroy and Bessie Public.

When Republicans make statements like "We want to eliminate the Department of Education," Leroy and Bessie Public hear, "Republicans don't care about education." When Republicans say, "We want to end all affirmative action programs," Leroy and Bessie think, "See, I knew they were racists and elitists." When Republicans say, "We need to build more prisons," Leroy and Bessie wonder, "Where are the programs to keep people out of prison?"

There is merit to the ideas of reducing the size and influence of the U.S. Department of Education and eliminating quota-based hiring mandates. The solutions to these issues, however, must be explained to the public in terms of the direct benefits derived from their implementation. Voters want to know how policy solutions will affect them personally, and not necessarily how many billions of dollars will be saved.

The public is much more likely to support changes in education policy if they are explained as allowing more local control of curriculums as opposed to eliminating an entire U.S. department because its bureaucrats are too liberal. "Education reform" is a nice term, but it is not the language of real people. Republicans need to say that they support strong, accountable public education. More citizens depend on public education than on private education. The fact that most teachers and administrators are more liberal than you does not mean you have to take a negative stance toward public education as an institution. Public education will be the only option for millions of children for a long time. We need to make it better.

Taxpayers will understand the logic behind cutting marginal tax rates on income when they see their personal incomes rise and increased job opportunities become available. The term "tax cut" does not resonate with all potential voters in the real world. Tax code replacement does resonate with small business owners frustrated with the compliance costs of filling out all their tax forms and watching valuable cash generated by their business being sucked out by unfair inventory and depreciation rules. Connecting with voters, like connecting with customers, requires a marketing and communications plan that adequately describes your superior product and inspires potential consumers to buy it.

Perception Is Reality, but Reality Matters

If the Republicans solve their brand identity problem, they will have an expanded voter base for decades. This will not be accomplished by simply loudly criticizing the Democrats during election time; it will require a deliberate plan between elections to inform and inspire voters.

Since the Contract with America stalled after Newt Gingrich left Congress, the Republicans have fallen back into the often used Democratic techniques of negative rhetoric and blame of the other party to win elections and to explain their policy agendas to voters. Republicans were put on the defensive by the Democrats most of the time. This contributed to gridlock in Congress and an expansion of the great divides and helped produce the close presidential elections of 2000 and 2004.

I understand that running a campaign is different in many ways from running a business. But political parties, like businesses, will never grow their voter base by promoting their product only to repeat customers and by constantly criticizing their competition. Businesses rely on their loyal repeat customers to keep the business going but are engaged every day in a battle to expand their customer base and show their competitors' customers why their product is better.

There is at least one big similarity between running a campaign and running a business. It's the thought, care, and attention that go into developing the message for the media campaign. For federal elections, this is critical and expensive. But not nearly enough attention and resources are expended between elections. Political campaigns are often focused primarily on securing the base and generating support for a candidate by telling the base all the reasons not to vote for the competing candidate. Businesses are focused primarily on spreading the positive news about their product or service. This in turn helps build a positive brand identity.

Millions of advertising dollars are spent by political campaigns each election cycle to portray competing candidates as the worst people on Earth, barely deserving of oxygen, let alone your vote. Truth is often the first casualty of an intense, negative campaign war, which leaves all but the dedicated base of political activists and observers confused and uninspired to vote.

The next casualties of an intense, negative campaign are the issues and, worse yet, the solutions a candidate proposes. Many candidates spend too little time discussing the issues and solutions to problems. Voters do not want to hear only how bad things are. They already know that. They want to hear credible hope that things can be better. Voters have always been inspired by hope, and they always will be.

Republicans also damage their brand identity when they repeatedly attack the Democratic Party and Democratic candidates. They are in effect attacking the party where many of the politically homeless once belonged. Many of the politically homeless have their political roots in the Democratic Party, and may still have family members who consider themselves Democrats. The politically homeless view attacks on the Democratic Party as an attack on some of the ideas they once supported. When Republicans focus their attacks on entities rather than specific issues and solutions, they alienate the politically homeless and a large pool of potentially Republican voters.

Since Democrats have co-opted most of the credit for civil rights gains, an attack on Democrats is viewed by many and especially Blacks as an attack on positive civil rights legislation. These attacks send a clear signal to the conservative base, but they send a negative signal to Blacks and other minority groups. Voters then question the racial sincerity of a political party that would attack the institutions they believe opened up opportunities and equal access for all citizens.

Most members of racial minorities support Democrat candidates, and many view the conservative policy agenda as hostile toward protection of their rights. The Republican Party could expand its base of supporters exponentially if it worked toward educating the public on its positive contributions to the civil rights struggle, coupled with the positive things it is doing even today. Potential voters would then be willing to listen to other policy solutions Republicans have to offer. In business you look for a sustainable point of difference between you and your competitors and then market and promote it until the cows come home.

Republicans will not capture the politically homeless and expand their base with the "build it and they will come" mentality or a strategy that employs the constant use of negative and divisive political rhetoric. Too many people do not pay attention to politics on a day-to-day basis, and they do not take time to connect political headlines to the facts. This is why it is so easy for perception to become reality in politics. Perception has to be deliberately managed.

Winning Voters Is Not Black and White . . . It's Green

At the heart of most people's version of the American Dream is a desire to achieve economic freedom. They also want to live in a nation that values the rule of law and protection of our moral foundations and to live in a nation that actively defends its citizens through military superiority from those who want to destroy our freedoms.

The version of economic freedom, like the version of the American Dream, varies from citizen to citizen. Achieving economic freedom could mean starting or expanding your own business, having enough money to invest or save for your children's future, or acquiring a level of financial security. Whatever your definition of economic freedom is, achieving it begins with controlling your own money.

The majority of U.S. citizens will never be able to control all their own money and work toward economic freedom as long as federal, state, and local governments continue to tax inheritance and incomes at disparate (or what government likes to call "progressive") rates and impose mountains of needless regulations and compliance costs on small businesses and large corporations.

The tax codes at all levels of government are used by politicians as tools for social engineering and to reward specific interests with credits for specific behaviors. The Social Security system has been abused for decades by Congress as a method to raise funds for members' favorite pork barrel projects in their districts to the point that the system will soon be fiscally insolvent. Instead of demonstrating leadership by addressing these problems and inequities head on, most of the solutions we hear about amount to slight cuts in marginal tax rates, more tax credits and deductions, and raising the Social Security retirement age to avoid having to make the politically dangerous decision of actually fixing the problems that undermine our nation's economic foundation.

If members of Congress were gamblers in Las Vegas, we would say they are playing with "house money." Unfortunately for us, we the people are the house and the money they play fast and loose with is our money, taken from us in the form of taxes every time we receive a paycheck, an investment dividend, an inheritance from our family members, or a Social Security check.

Our potential for achieving economic freedom is diminished further every day that we do not demand a complete replacement of the federal tax code and a complete restructuring of the Social Security system. The majority of individual citizens will never be able to achieve economic freedom and their American Dream as long as they are not allowed to control every penny of the money they earn.

Today, U.S. citizens from every demographic background are graduating from trade schools, colleges and universities, and graduate school programs at a rate their parents and grandparents likely thought impossible. People from all backgrounds are using the power of the diploma to climb the corporate ladder and start their own businesses. They are purchasing cars, condominiums, and homes at levels their parents only dreamed of. They are saving and investing for their futures and their children's futures and building their own wealth.

At the same time, millions of citizens who have achieved first-generation wealth are receiving an education in the famous School of Hard Knocks. Each time they receive a paycheck and see how much is deducted off the top in the form of payroll taxes, find out that they have to sell the family business because they cannot afford to pay the inheritance taxes, or find out that this year they have to pay the arcane and insane Alternative Minimum Tax, they realize the staggering financial impositions placed on U.S. citizens by their own representatives in government.

Congressional Republicans must follow President Bush's lead and act immediately to institute the reforms necessary to allow greater access to economic freedom for all citizens. In future elections the politically homeless will support candidates who can articulate common sense economic policies that reduce government control of our money and regulations on small businesses. The politically homeless will also be looking for candidates who will not start to back-peddle as soon as they take office. The politically homeless are looking for real leaders.

In future generations, a higher percentage of citizens will be able to build wealth because of increased access to educational opportunities, employment opportunities, and instruments for financial investment. They will demand that government fiscal policies support a modern economic infrastructure and that these policies represent present-day realities, not the economic realities of 1913, 1935, or 1965.

One political reality that will ring as true in the future as it does today is that congressional Democrats will attempt to block any economic policies that increase the opportunity for all citizens to achieve economic freedom. Democrats simply cannot control our lives if they do not control our pocketbooks.

Republicans must seize on the current opportunity they have for leadership on economic policies and enact the reforms that will demonstrate to loyal Republicans, curious Democrats, and the politically homeless that they are serious about our nation's economic future.

If Republicans are to win new voters now and in the future, they must fight for those votes with the assumption that every citizen is a potential supporter of their policy agenda. Secondly, they must assume that voters are smart enough to get it when they say it the right way at the right time. Thirdly, Republicans must keep the media and the public focused on the big issues and the aggressive solutions.

Controlling the national policy agenda requires winning presidential and congressional elections. Republican campaign strategy cannot rely forever solely on the votes of White conservatives. Republicans must cast a wider net and attract the support of racial minorities who will comprise the growing numbers of those citizens willing and able to accumulate wealth. The good news is that Republicans do not have to change their ideology and pander to specific groups as the Democrats so often do. They just have to do a much better job of telling their story.

In addition to the president and Republican members of Congress, responsibility for helping all citizens achieve economic freedom also falls on our nation's religious leaders. Our nation's religious institutions and houses of worship are for millions of citizens the primary source of information on cultural and political affairs. Religious organizations are often a highly influential source of information regarding which political candidates and policies their members will support.

Contrary to the advice of most mothers everywhere, politics and religion do mix, and we should feel comfortable discussing both topics. Politics and religion are not mutually exclusive issues. Those who want to destroy this nation want us to think they are. Anyone who takes the time to read the founding documents of our country can conclude this reality for him or herself. Our moral foundations provide the inspirational basis of our great country and are the precursor for achieving personal economic success and the maintenance of the rule of law.

As a primary influence in the lives of millions of U.S. citizens, religious leaders and organizations have a duty to educate their congregations on the impact of political issues in their lives. Unfortunately, too many religious organizations and religious leaders are either reluctant to educate their congregations on the political issues and the political process, or they act as overly zealous surrogates of a particular political party in an attempt to keep their members chained to tradition and the political ideologies of their ancestors.

Still other pastors are gun-shy of the line between what is permitted according to the tax code for nonprofit organizations and what is considered political. As a result, they play it safe and do nothing. This is yet another example of how the tax code interferes with doing what is in the best interest of people. Replacing the income tax code with a national sales tax would eliminate this problem.

In his book *Scam: How the Black Leadership Exploits Black America*, Rev. Jesse Lee Peterson discusses at length how many Black pastors and the so-called Black leaders have forged a partnership with the Democratic Party that is now ingrained in much of Black social, religious, and political culture. Rev. Peterson writes, "These pastors have often been responsible for leading their congregations astray. Instead of looking to God, they are taught to look to other gods—the god of government programs or the god of the so-called black leader. This puts most Blacks right in the pocket of the Democratic Party, which has become a god for many as well" (59).

Rev. Peterson's insightful and eye-opening book details the scam perpetrated on Blacks by the so-called Black leaders, such as Jesse Jackson, Julian Bond, and Joseph Lowery, since the death of Dr. Martin Luther King Jr. For more than forty years they have taken advantage of the trust Blacks place in their spiritual leaders. The self-appointed Black leaders, in conjunction with some unfortunately unscrupulous church leaders, have convinced many Blacks that White racism is the cause of their problems and that support of the Democratic Party's liberal social and economic policies is the key to lifting one's self out of poverty.

Rev. Peterson convincingly makes the case that more Black pastors across the country need to get off the Democratic plantation and engage their congregations in an honest, educational discussion of the most important social and economic political issues. They must discontinue advocating the politics of groupthink founded and still mired in the civil rights struggles of the 1960s and instead focus on the issues of elementary economics, personal responsibility, education, and economic freedom. Black pastors have an enormous influence on their congregations and the ability to help end the cycles of government dependence and economic slavery so prevalent today in many Black communities.

Religious leaders from all denominations also possess the ability to teach their congregations how to organize at the grassroots level of political involvement and influence social and economic policies. One does not have to tell people how to vote, but one can help people become a more informed voter. The potential for positive change is enormous if church leaders and their congregations put behind them the notion that politics and religion are not related.

Despite the negative rhetoric we hear every day from liberals, economic opportunity and prosperity are available to every citizen who possesses dreams and the willingness to work hard to pursue them. Most citizens realize that, even in the presence of government policies that restrict our ability to build wealth. The only barrier to economic success is personal initiative and determination.

More and more people no longer view issues and candidates through race-colored glasses or vote based solely on their religious affiliation and past tradition. President Reagan demonstrated in the presidential elections of 1980 and 1984 that Republican candidates can win the support of traditional Democrat voters with common sense economic policies. The success of President Reagan's fiscal policies allowed millions of citizens to build first-generation financial security and wealth and in the process created lifetime supporters of the Republican Party. I am one of them.

Winning voters is not black and white . . . *it's green.*

History and the Facts Are on Your Side— Use Them!

In fighting the war to protect our nation's economic and moral foundations, the Republican Party has on its side the unparalleled weapons of history and facts. It was members of the Republican Party who educated the nation on the horrors of slavery and who fought and died in a war to guarantee slavery's end. It was Republicans who led the fights in Congress in the 1950s and 1960s to guarantee basic civil rights for all citizens of the United States. It was conservative fiscal policy under the administration of President Ronald Reagan that set in motion the longest peacetime economic growth in our nation's history.

Whether the fight has been for the end of slavery, for the protection of the guaranteed constitutional freedoms for all citizens, or for economic policies that lessen government control of our money and allow all citizens to work toward economic freedom, it has always been Republicans who have been on the right side of history and have been relentless advocates for the policies we know in our hearts to be right.

Republicans must consider it their daily mission to educate the public on the positive effects of a conservative policy agenda, and they must remain resolute when advocating their policy agenda in Congress. Republicans must continue to expand their customer base and give the politically homeless reasons to support Republican candidates and their policies—and not just more reasons to oppose Democrats. Republicans must continue to explain their positive policy agenda in terms of the human benefits derived by enactment of their policies.

Republicans can no longer afford to lose ground in the battle for the votes of the politically homeless to Democrats who fight with the weapons of distortion, negative rhetoric, and outright lies. Fortunately, the prevailing conventional wisdom that members of the politically homeless decide which political party to support based on the number of Blacks or Hispanics, Catholics or Jews one sees standing behind a given party's leaders is mistaken. Support for the Republican Party is increasing among members of all demographics based on the positive facts of the conservative policy agenda.

In the 2004 campaign cycle, numerous conservative 527 organizations such as America's PAC, Council for Better Government, and Hispanics Together paid for tens of thousands of television and radio advertisements on Black radio and Spanish language media outlets in the battleground states to inform voters on the truth about President Bush's policy agenda and to counter the negative claims made by Democrats.

According to Richard Nadler, president of America's PAC, conservative 527 groups ran twelve thousand advertisements on Spanish language media in support of the conservative message and Republican candidates. In the states where the advertisements ran, President Bush secured more than 47 percent of the Hispanic vote, compared to an average of 36 percent in the states where the groups did not place advertisements.

Bush also increased his support among Black voters in five of the battleground states in which America's PAC placed advertisements. He received 12 to 16 percent support from Black voters in Florida, Ohio, Pennsylvania, Wisconsin, and

Minnesota. These numbers were significantly higher than Bush's 11 percent support among Blacks nationally.

The advertisements placed by conservative organizations to tell the truth about the Republican policy agenda to Black and Hispanic voters focused on numerous conservative issues, including protection of traditional marriage, tax reform, school choice, abortion, strong national defense, and faith-based social services. The significant rise in support among Black and Hispanic voters for President Bush's policy agenda clearly indicates that when voters hear the truth, versus distortion and lies, they are willing to support conservative candidates.

It is also important to note that the vast majority of issue education and voter outreach efforts directed toward racial minorities has been done by organizations not directly affiliated with the Republican Party. The Republican Party itself must demonstrate that it is willing to use its vast resources to reach out to minority voters and educate them on the realities of the conservative policy agenda. The party cannot continue to remain "missing in action" from the battle for the votes of all citizens.

There is still much more work to do. In the absence of a dedicated effort to educate the public on the realities of the Republican agenda, the perception still exits among people like Scotty and others like him that the Grand Old Party cannot relate to the struggles of common folk. I have a suggestion:

The Republican Party should change the meaning of that old acronym from *Grand Old Party* to *Government Of the People.* Government Of the People means that Republicans believe people make better decisions for themselves than government. It means they believe people know how to spend their hard-earned money better than out-of-touch bureaucrats in Washington. It means they believe people want a fair chance to succeed, pursue their American Dream, and achieve economic freedom. Government Of the People should become the new slogan of the Republican Party and a welcome sign for any American who believes in themselves and a bright future for this great country.

In 1858, President Abraham Lincoln stated in his "House Divided" speech,

> Our cause, then, must be entrusted to, and conducted by, its own undoubted friends—those whose hands are free, whose hearts are in the work—who do care for the result. Two years ago the Republicans of the nation mustered over thirteen thousand strong.
>
> We did this under the single impulse of resistance to a common danger, with every external circumstance against us. Of strange, discordant, and even hostile elements, we gathered from the four winds, and formed and fought the battle through, under the constant hot fire of a disciplined, proud, and pampered enemy. Did we brave all them to falter now? Now, when that same enemy is wavering, dissevered, and belligerent? The result is not doubtful.
>
> We shall not fail—if we stand firm, we shall not fail. Wise counsels may accelerate, or mistakes delay it, but, sooner or later, the victory is sure to come.

President Lincoln's encouragement to fellow Republicans to continue the fight against Democrats who opposed the abolition of slavery should likewise serve as a rallying cry today to Republicans. They should pursue aggressive policy solutions that guarantee economic freedom for all citizens and protection of our nation's moral foundations, despite the difficulty. It is our collective right and responsibility.

Earth to Republicans! Voters are smarter than you think. History and the facts are on your side. Use them!

Voters Are Smarter Than Republicans Think

- Many of the ideologically moderate but politically homeless found a temporary home in the Republican Party in 2004, but Republicans still cannot convince many of these temporary residents to identify themselves as Republicans. The majority of Black, Latino, Asian, and ideologically moderate voters have still not been persuaded by the Republican Party to embrace the Republican policy agenda.
- The top three issues for voters in 2004 were moral values, the status of the economy and job growth, and the global war on terrorism. Of these three issues, President Bush received overwhelming support from those who view moral values and the war on terrorism as most important.

Republicans Have a Brand Identity Problem

- Whereas the Democratic Party has an ideology problem, the Republican Party has a brand identity problem.
- When people stop and really look at the primary tenets of what it means to be a Republican, they quickly realize that they are more ideologically aligned with the Republican Party. But they quickly go back to their perception of the party and denounce any formal affiliation. That's the weakness of the brand.
- Connecting with voters, like connecting with customers, requires a marketing and communications plan that adequately describes your superior product and inspires potential consumers to buy it.

Perception Is Reality, but Reality Matters
- If the Republicans solve their brand identity problem, they will have an expanded voter base for decades. This will not be accomplished by simply loudly criticizing the Democrats during election time; it will require a deliberate plan between elections to inform and inspire voters.
- Republicans damage their brand identity when they repeatedly attack the Democratic Party and Democrat candidates. They are in effect attacking the party where many of the politically homeless once belonged. In addition, since Democrats have co-opted most of the credit for civil rights gains, an attack on Democrats is viewed by many and especially Blacks as an attack on positive civil rights legislation.
- Perception has to be deliberately managed. This is true for business and it is true for politics.

Winning Voters Is Not Black and White . . . It's Green
- At the heart of most people's version of the American Dream is a desire to achieve economic freedom.
- Our potential for achieving economic freedom is diminished further every day that we do not demand a complete replacement of the federal tax code and a complete restructuring of the Social Security system.
- Republicans must seize on the current opportunity they have for leadership on economic policies and enact the reforms that will demonstrate to loyal Republicans, curious Democrats, and the politically homeless that they are serious about our nation's economic future.

History and the Facts Are on Your Side—Use Them!
- In fighting the war to protect our nation's economic and moral foundations, as well as individual liberties and civil rights, the Republican Party has on its side the unparalleled weapons of history and facts.

- The Republican Party should change the meaning of that old GOP acronym from *Grand Old Party* to *Government Of the People*. Only with this change of common perception will the Republicans gain the trust of the politically homeless, who now don't always fully identify their traditionally conservative values with their natural political affiliation as Republicans.

Chapter 5

We are *All* in the Same Boat Now

The terrorist attacks on September 11, 2001, reminded us that we are a nation of individuals who share many of the same hopes and dreams. We are all pursuing economic freedom and our versions of the American Dream, yet we share in the consequences of political decisions that either strengthen or further weaken our economic foundations. In a crisis we unite. In times of prolonged prosperity we fight among ourselves like cats and dogs. Terrorism is a crisis. We must unite behind both the global war on terrorism waged by enemies in foreign lands and the war against our economic foundations waged by enemies of economic freedom within.

Will the twenty-first century be a time that sees the American public consumed with fear and doubt? Fear of another, devastating terrorist attack, and doubt in our ability to enact aggressive policy solutions? Or will history judge this as a century filled with inspired unity and hope—a nation united behind defeating the terrorists who want to forever alter our way of life and a nation filled with hope in its ability to protect its borders and achieve economic freedom for all citizens?

Terrorists Want to Kill All of Us

In April 2002, former Israeli prime minister Benjamin Netanyahu delivered a captivating speech to the U.S. Senate in which he called on his lifetime of experiences in confronting the evils of terrorist states and encouraged the United States to remain resolute in the global war against terrorism. Portions of that speech are included below.

> I have come here to voice what I believe is an urgently needed reminder: that the war on terror can be won with clarity and courage or lost with confusion and vacillation.
>
> This moral and strategic clarity was applied with devastating effect to the Taliban regime in Afghanistan that supported Al Qaeda terrorism.
>
> Soon after the war began, the American victory over the forces of terror in Afghanistan brought to light the third principle in the war on terror— namely, that the best way to defeat terror is to defeat it. At first, this seemingly trite observation was not fully understood. Contrary to popular belief, the motivating force behind terror is neither desperation nor destitution. It is hope—the hope of terrorists systematically brainwashed by the ideologies who manipulate them that their savagery will break the will of their enemies and help them achieve their objectives—political, religious, or otherwise.
>
> Faced with the quintessential terrorist regime of our time—a regime that both harbors and perpetuates terror on an unimaginable scale—the free world is muddling its principles, losing its nerve, and thereby endangering the successful prosecution of this war.

The question many in my country are now asking is this: Will America apply its principles consistently and win this war, or will it selectively abandon those principles and thereby ultimately lose the war?

If not destroyed, this madness will strike in your buses, in your supermarkets, in your pizza parlors, in your cafes. Eventually, these human bombs will supplement their murderous force with suitcases equipped with devices of mass death that could make the horrors of September 11 pale by comparison.

That is why there is no alternative to winning this war without delay. No part of the terrorist network can be left intact. For if not fully eradicated, like the most malignant cancer, it will regroup and attack again with even greater ferocity. Only by dismantling the entire network will we be assured of victory.

But to assure that this evil does not reemerge a decade or two from now, we must not merely uproot terror, but also plant the seeds of freedom.

Because only under tyranny can a diseased totalitarian mindset be widely cultivated. This totalitarian mindset, which is essential for terrorists to suspend the normal rules that govern a man's conscience and prevent him from committing these grisly acts, does not breed in a climate of democracy and freedom.

The open debate and plurality of ideas that buttress all genuine democracies and the respect for human rights and the sanctity of life that are the shared values of all free societies are a permanent antidote to the poison that the sponsors of terror seek to inject into the minds of their recruits.

History has entrusted this nation with carrying the torch of freedom. And time and time again, through both war and peace, America has carried that torch with courage and with honor, combining a might the world has never known with a sense of justice that no power in history has possessed.

Prime Minister Netanyahu's opening sentence is a strategic declaration: "That the war on terror can be won with clarity and courage or lost with confusion and vacillation."

His impassioned plea to the U.S. Senate and all U.S. citizens was borne from direct interaction with terrorist states and their leaders as a citizen, soldier, elected official, and statesman, and from years of observing the unique, humanitarian nature of U.S. foreign policy. Netanyahu understands that the U.S. does not seek to overthrow nations and impose dictatorial or totalitarian regimes on conquered peoples, a la the former Soviet Union. On the contrary, U.S. foreign policy has generally focused on bringing freedom and the prospect of self-government to oppressed people throughout the world.

Netanyahu's speech was not aimed specifically at Republicans, nor was it targeted to Democrats. It was aimed at all U.S. citizens who might question for even a second the necessity of waging war against terrorist networks on their home turf. There can be no doubt that terrorists all over the globe seek to disrupt and destroy our way of life, our values, and our freedoms. Generations of Americans have fought and died to protect our values and freedoms, and we must continue to do so when we are attacked.

Global terrorism did not begin on September 11, 2001, nor did our efforts to combat it. Most Americans did not pay much attention to terrorism, however, because terrorist attacks on U.S. soil were rare and certainly not of the magnitude of the World Trade Center bombings. September 11, 2001, was our biggest wakeup call to the threat of global terror since the Japanese attacked Pearl Harbor in 1941.

Following the September 11 attacks, churches were packed across the country every Sunday. People were calling others they had never met before "brother" or "sister." An unmistakable sense of patriotism and pride in our great nation filled football stadiums, baseball stadiums, and anywhere people rallied in support of the United States and our military personnel.

Fear has a uniting influence, but as Americans we sometimes quickly forget that the factors still exist that once caused us to fear. It did not take long after President Bush committed troops to wipe out the Taliban in Afghanistan, and set in motion policies that would eventually allow Afghan citizens to hold their own elections and select their own leaders, for congressional Democrats and some squishy Republicans to restart their partisan bickering by complaining that the president rushed to war and was going it alone without support of other nations.

There are always people who believe the U.S. should never go to war. They believe that somehow we can reason with totalitarian dictators who have no qualms about strapping suicide bombs to women and children under the ruse of martyrdom. The fact is, no sane American ever desires to go to war prior to exhausting all available diplomatic options. War is ugly, war breaks up families, and war causes many children to grow up without a parent.

War, however, is sometimes the only solution to ending or preventing destruction of American lives and attacks on U.S. soil. The preeminent charge of the U.S. government is to defend its borders and its citizens. Those who oppose U.S. prosecution of the global war on terrorism following the attacks of September 11, 2001, offer no reasonable alternative and obviously have an agenda separate from protecting U.S. interests, freedoms, and lives.

Clearly, all aspects of the war on terrorism have not gone as planned. For example, the intelligence provided by our CIA and FBI to the president and other leaders has not always been accurate. The U.S. military, however, has achieved in a relatively short amount of time what no other nation has ever accomplished—the imprisonment or killing of thousands of the worlds' leading terrorists and their leaders. Military personnel have secured much evidence of terrorists' plans to manufacture weapons of mass destruction, including nuclear and chemical weapons. Successful elections have been held in Afghanistan and

Iraq. Girls are now allowed to attend schools in those countries, and people no longer live in constant fear of their own leaders. For the first time in their lives, people in the Middle East have hope for the future.

The strength of our nation, the greatest country on Earth, is that it has always represented a beacon of hope for the entire world. In 1630, upon the deck of a boat off the coast of Massachusetts, John Winthrop said, "We will be as a city upon a hill. The eyes of all people are upon us, so that if we deal falsely with our God in this work we have undertaken and so cause Him to withdraw His present help from us, we shall be made a story and a byword throughout the world."

There have been some dark moments in our nation's history, but because of our freedoms, not despite them, our nation persevered, became stronger, and we understood a little more why God created this beautiful land and gave us the opportunity to live here.

I have read recently some of the chilling and frightening accounts of the brutality toward slaves during the horrible time in our history when slavery was permitted. Often a Black man or woman was brutally killed for no reason at all.

Growing up in Atlanta during the 1950s and 1960s, I can still remember the painted rules on the public buses that said, "Colored seat from the rear. Whites seat from the front." It was humiliating and demeaning, especially when the bus got full and the Blacks were supposed to get up and yield their seat to any White person. During segregation, a Black person was beaten or killed for getting out of line toward a White person, even if the accusation was baseless.

Emmett Till, a fourteen-year-old Black boy from Chicago, was visiting relatives in Mississippi during summer 1955. While on a trip to a grocery store with his cousins, he allegedly whistled at a White woman, who went home and told her husband. Several nights later, the woman's husband and others kidnapped Emmett from his relatives' home in the middle of the night. They severely beat him, shot him, and threw his body in a nearby river. They were later charged with the murder of young Emmett Till and faced seemingly insurmountable evidence of their guilt. The jury deliberated less than an hour, however, and acquitted all the accused.

Several months later, a journalist covering the case offered the woman's husband and his accomplice money to tell the true story of their involvement in the murder of Emmett Till. The two could no longer be prosecuted for a crime of which they had been acquitted, so they told the reporter in detail how they had beaten and killed Emmett. Their story was published in 1956.

Soon after the true story of the murder of Emmett Till became public, the two men responsible for his brutal murder were forced out of their community and moved elsewhere. Young Emmett Till became an icon for the civil rights movement across the country. Justice may not always prevail in the courtroom, but sometimes it prevails in different ways.

Justice may also take a long time, but justice usually prevails in a free society. On Sunday, September 15, 1963, four little Black girls were killed while attending Sunday school class when a bomb exploded at the Sixteenth Street Baptist Church in Birmingham, Alabama. Denise McNair, Addie Mae Collins, Carole Robertson, and Cynthia Wesley, like Emmett Till before them, came to symbolize the struggles of Blacks in the segregated South.

Then-FBI Director J. Edgar Hoover declined to investigate the case, saying that the possibility for a conviction was remote. In 1971 the Alabama attorney general's office reopened the case, and by 1977 a man named Robert Edward Chambliss was convicted of one count of murder in Carol McNair's death. In 1980 the U.S. Department of Justice released a report stating FBI Director Hoover had blocked evidence that could have been used in the investigation into the bombing.

The FBI in 1997 reopened its investigation. In May 2000 two more men, Thomas Blanton and Bobby Frank Cherry, surrendered after an Alabama grand jury indicted them on first-degree murder charges for their roles in the bombing. One year later, a jury found Thomas Blanton guilty of four counts of first-degree murder and sentenced him to life imprisonment. Bobby Frank Cherry was in a Texas prison serving time for a separate crime.

Most of us have moved past racial hatred and understand that we are all God's children, blessed with the ability to live in America and pursue economic freedom, and charged with protecting those freedoms our nation's Founding Fathers declared, fought, and died for. We know from the terrorists' own words that they hate all of us and our freedoms: Republicans and Democrats; Blacks, Whites, Latinos, and Asians; Christians and Jews.

Now is not the time for the petty, divisive backbiting waged every day by congressional Democrats. We must stand together on the issues that transcend partisan politics, as Americans stood together following the attack on Pearl Harbor. Support of President Bush and our military should not be partisan as they prosecute the war on terrorism. Otherwise, the terrorists will be victorious in their mission to instill fear, divide, and destroy our great nation. Former Ambassador Andrew Young echoed this sentiment when he stated, "Foreign policy must be bipartisan. The enemy is violence and chaos in regions critical to global survival" ("Elections are Iraq's best hope," *Atlanta Journal-Constitution*, 28 January 2005).

Unfortunately, liberal media outlets and Democratic officials continue to bash President Bush and our military personnel for their successes in fighting to end terrorism across the globe. They claim the U.S. is less safe under President Bush's leadership, that we have no reason to fight a portion of the war in Iraq, and that the elected leaders of liberated nations are "puppets" of the U.S.

Essentially, the media and Democrats are upset that a Republican happened to be occupying the White House when we were attacked and began to fight back. They cannot stand the fact that President Bush and our military personnel have led and waged an incredibly successful war against the madmen of the Middle East who hate all Americans. Fortunately, the liberal media and Democrats have been unsuccessful in weakening the resolve of the majority of Americans to support the fight against terror on terror's breeding ground. What their caustic, divisive rhetoric has accomplished, however, is increased infighting and partisanship among the public in a time of war—a time when we should be allied as a nation against outside threats.

Prime Minister Netanyahu stated to the U.S. Senate that "The motivating force behind terrorists . . . is hope—the hope of terrorists systematically brainwashed by the ideologies who manipulate them that their savagery will break the will of their enemies and help them achieve their objectives—political, religious, or otherwise." Americans also share a hope—a hope in their ability to rise up out of any adversity they were born into or find themselves in and achieve all their dreams.

Our shared hopes and dreams will not be torn asunder by a network of murderous madmen outside our country bent on destroying the beacon of hope that shines throughout the world. Democrats and the liberal media must not be allowed to plant the seeds of doubt from within our nation that destroy hope in our abilities, weaken the morale of the public and military personnel, and divide rather than unite us in defense of our shared freedoms.

The terrorists want to kill *all* of us—even Democrats.

Economic Slavery for All

As a great-great-grandson of slaves, I welcome those of you who are not descendants of slavery during America's darkest period in history to the "new slavery." Not the slavery of one man owning another as his property, but economic slavery—the slavery to a government bureaucracy that is out of control, except to control a disproportionate share of the property of one's labor. To paraphrase Abraham Lincoln as he contested the slavery of his day, "You work and toil and earn bread, and someone else eats it."

It is exceedingly difficult for someone to escape systemic poverty, to start a small business, maintain a business, or pass a business on to one's workers or family members. To make matters worse, if you are able to escape poverty or if you are just surviving paycheck to paycheck, you then have to constantly contend with a threatening, confiscatory, unfair, and overly complex tax code that tries to negate your economic progress all the way to the grave.

Numerous free market and government-controlled factors affect the strength of the U.S. economy, including interest and inflation rates, barriers to trade of U.S. goods abroad, and the price of foreign oil. Without question, however, three government programs—the federal tax code, the Social Security system, and the Medicare program form the basis of our economic infrastructure. The tax code, Social Security, and Medicare have the greatest effect on the opportunities for people to achieve economic freedom or remain forever chained to the U.S. government in economic slavery.

The federal tax code, Social Security, and Medicare, enacted in 1913, 1935, and 1965, respectively, are the three pillars that support the nation's economic infrastructure. More visible and easily manipulated factors like interest rates and trade agreements can certainly affect the economy's short-term successes or failures. An inextricable relationship exists, though, between our personal and business lives and the onerous tax code, our retirement plans and the health care system. The relationship illustrates the level to which our personal and professional lives are controlled, whether we notice it or not, by these three pillars.

The primary fault with our economic infrastructure is that it was pieced together throughout the last century using assumptions that are now long invalid. The authors of the tax code, Social Security system, and the Medicare program could not and did not foresee the impact of the United States on the global economy, the size and influence of the baby boomer generation, or the myriad advances in technology and their impact on all facets of our lives.

In addition, the dynamics of wealth building and individual achievement have changed dramatically in just the last twenty years. Upward mobility from generation to generation is the norm. Today's white-collar workers and small business owners are the sons and daughters of yesterday's blue-collar union members. Women now make up a significant percentage of the workplace. Racial minorities are more upwardly mobile and represented in every aspect of corporate America. More than half of the U.S. workforce owns financial investments such as stocks and bonds. More young people have college educations and advanced degrees than ever before. The marketplace for goods and services, ideas and innovations is global in scale. Perhaps most important, history has shown us the inefficiencies of centralized government programs and command economies. Yet, due to political pressures and a lack of leadership in most corners of state and federal government, we continue to place band-aids on an infrastructure that requires major reconstructive surgery.

The current federal income tax code is an eight-million-word mess, and it cannot be reformed or restructured. It creates disadvantages for families wondering how to pay for their children's education, for small businesses struggling to pay the bills and meet payroll, for multinational businesses trying to compete in the global marketplace against lower-priced goods from foreign countries, and for any U.S. citizen working hard every day to achieve the American Dream. No amount of tinkering with a portion of the tax code is going to fix it. It is too complicated. It is too unfair and inefficient. It discourages people from working harder to achieve upward economic mobility, which destroys hope and opportunity.

On July 1, 1943, the federal government began an immoral program that would forever change the way Americans think (or, in this case, *don't* think) about taxation. That is the day the federal government enacted what we know of as "automatic withholding." Prior to this date, people were responsible for sending the Internal Revenue Service a check by April 15 each year for the amount of taxes owed on their prior year's income. People knew exactly how much they were paying Uncle Sam for the government services he provided.

The federal government, however, was not pleased with this situation. It took the Federal Treasury too long to get your money. Automatic withholding was designed as a way to fill the federal coffers every month and to mask the true cost of ever-escalating federal spending. Congress explained to the people that, since the U.S. was busy fighting World War II, automatic withholding was necessary to fund the war effort in a timely fashion. Congress also promised the public that automatic withholding would end as soon as the war was over. That war ended sixty years ago.

Of course, taxes are still automatically withheld from your paycheck. Automatic withholding contributes to the economic slavery of working people because it keeps them ignorant about how much of their income they actually pay in taxes. Americans have simply been conditioned over time to accept the fact that their true amount of income is their take-home pay, which is roughly the amount they receive in each paycheck. Adding fuel to this fire, the federal government annually withholds too much of your money from each paycheck. Some people always seem overjoyed that they get back a big check each year from the Federal Treasury. Instead, they should be outraged. They forget that it's their money in the first place!

Automatic withholding is nothing short of immoral on the basis that it keeps people ignorant of the true cost of government and the amount of taxes they actually pay. In addition, the federal government, in its eternal arrogance, annually takes more from your paycheck than you actually owe in taxes! In effect, you are giving the federal government an interest free loan each year. And you are supposed to be happy to get *your* money back!

The federal tax code must be replaced, and it must be replaced with a national retail sales tax, also known as the FairTax. The FairTax is a federal retail sales tax that replaces the entire federal income and Social Security tax systems, including personal, gift, estate, capital gains, alternative minimum, Social Security/Medicare, self-employment, and corporate taxes. The FairTax allows Americans to keep 100 percent of their paychecks (minus any state income taxes), ends corporate taxes and compliance costs hidden in the retail cost of goods and services, and fully funds the federal government.

Several commissions over the last twenty years, including the one I served on in 1995 (the National Commission on Economic Growth and Tax Reform), have all concluded that a replacement tax system should satisfy six principles. First, it should promote economic growth by reducing marginal tax rates and eliminating the tax bias against savings and investments. Second, it should promote fairness by having one tax rate and eliminating all loopholes, preferences and special deductions, credits and exclusions. Third, it should be simple and understandable. Simplicity would dramatically reduce compliance costs and allow people to truly comprehend their actual tax burden. Fourth, it should be neutral rather than allowing misguided officials to manipulate and micromanage our economy by favoring some at the expense of others. Fifth, it should be visible so it clearly conveys the true cost of government and so people would not be subjected to hidden changes in the tax law. Sixth, it should be stable rather than changing every year or two so people can better plan their businesses and their lives.

The FairTax satisfies *all* six criteria. Period. Why has it not been enacted? The answer is Congress wants economic slavery for all. Where are the affirmative action advocates? Where is the American Civil Liberties Union (ACLU)? Where is the NAACP? The answer is a disgusting "They don't get it!"

The Social Security system is nearing bankruptcy due to decades of mismanagement, a flawed structure, and a lack of leadership and political will in Congress for meaningful change. What is worse, we have known for more than twenty-five years that the system is destined for failure. Yet, every year, Congress shirks its duty to address the problems in Social Security and instead has implemented such preposterous solutions as raising taxes on Social Security benefits (also known as "double dipping") and increasing every year the retirement age for benefits.

Fifty years ago, there were sixteen workers to support every person on Social Security. Today there are only 3.3 workers to support every beneficiary. By the time our children and grandchildren, those just entering the workforce today, turn 65, there will be only two workers supporting each person on Social Security.

The current Social Security system cannot afford to pay promised benefits to our children and grandchildren without enormous tax increases because *the system is broken.* The Social Security system was not designed to be the sole provider of retirement benefits for our seniors. Nor was it designed to account for the large baby boomer generation or to be a source of funds for Congress to raid to spend on one pork barrel project after another.

We can no longer afford to pour more tax dollars into the broken Social Security structure. The Social Security system, like the federal tax code, will keep workers in economic slavery for as long as the program continues in its current form. Younger workers of every demographic will never see a penny of the money automatically withheld from them each month. Because of the discrepancies in age expectancies, minority workers currently nearing retirement will be lucky to receive a few years of low benefits because Social Security continues to increase the retirement age.

The system must be changed to address current realities in the United States: the large baby boomer generation, which will soon reach retirement age; the proliferation and accessibility of personal retirement plans to most working citizens; and the known fact that our children and grandchildren will likely see none of the benefits they have paid into the system.

We know how to fix the Social Security system. The model of a system of personal retirement accounts was successfully installed in the country of Chile in 1980. It has worked ever since!

Three fundamental changes must be made to the Social Security system if we are to keep the promise of benefits to our seniors and the soon-to-be-retiring baby boomers, while providing more benefit options to future generations. First, we must establish a system of optional personal retirement accounts. Personal retirement accounts will provide workers ownership of monies paid into the system, choice in the level of risk and potential return on investment, and the opportunity to build a nest egg for their retirement and an inheritance for their families. Currently, nearly all citizens have access to personal retirement accounts either privately or through their place of employment. Personal retirement accounts provide their owners a long-term rate of return that the current Social Security system can never match. Individual citizens—not the federal government—will have the power to decide how a portion of their Social Security contribution is invested, and individuals will have the opportunity to benefit from the gains of long-term investing.

Second, benefits must no longer be reduced based on secondary or supplemental incomes. Many seniors take part-time jobs during their retirement years to supplement their retirement benefits or simply to stay active and to provide others their years of experience. Unfortunately, the current Social Security system penalizes retirees who choose to work during retirement by reducing benefits they earned. The current system treats retirees no different than welfare beneficiaries. This aspect of the Social Security system is simply ridiculous. Retired seniors who spent a lifetime contributing to society and paying into the system should not be treated like younger welfare recipients who are still in their working years. In addition, retired seniors can provide to others a lifetime of experience and talents. They are robbed of this opportunity under the penalty of losing their benefits.

Third, seniors must be allowed to leave the balance of their personal accounts to their widows, children, and any other heirs they designate. It is unconscionable that those currently receiving benefits receive a near negative rate of return on their money, are taxed twice on their benefits, and upon their death the balance of their earned benefits is returned to the system. "Massa" and "Uncle Sam" appear to be the same thing. Social Security benefits are monies earned during the retirees' working years, and retirees should be able to leave the balance of their accounts to their families, not to "Massa."

The health care system in the United States is severely sick. I am not talking about the doctors and health care professionals who find a way to do their jobs despite bureaucratic barriers and the fear of frivolous lawsuits. I am referring to all the influences by the federal government, federal regulatory agencies, state governments, state regulatory agencies, insurance companies, and trial lawyers. Seemingly every entity imaginable except the patient and the doctor exert a degree of influence over health care policy, health care delivery, and liability laws. All of these bodies, working at times in concert and at times as adversaries, have produced an over-priced and over-regulated system that prices millions of citizens out of the health insurance market while creating a paperwork and compliance nightmare for health care providers.

The health care system is made worse because of the treatment of insurance premiums in the tax code. Businesses can deduct premiums they pay for employee health care benefits as a business expense, but individual citizens cannot deduct the premiums they pay when they purchase their own health care insurance. That's part of the problem. Allowing businesses and individuals the same tax treatment in the tax code, and expanding the use of health savings accounts, will allow free market principles to help bring runaway costs under control. The principle is a simple one. People will spend their money more wisely than they will spend somebody else's money.

Decisions on treatment options and pricing are not made between patients and their doctors and are not based on free market principles. Instead, bureaucrats tucked safely away in Washington, D.C. and in our state capitals crunch numbers, contort statistics, and cavort with insurance company lobbyists to ensure that patients receive some predetermined level of care that is often inadequate or even unnecessary. Meanwhile, litigious lawyers wait with bated breath outside operating rooms to sue a doctor or even the whole hospital for negligence or malpractice.

The Medicare program is facing insolvency as baby boomers approach retirement. The recently enacted drug benefit only compounds the problem. It burdens future generations with trillions of dollars of new debt and jeopardizes the existing drug coverage of many working and retired Americans. The costs associated with millions of Americans lacking health care insurance, increased regulations on insurance companies, increased costs to the individual states to administer Medicaid programs, and trial lawyers who abuse the legal system with frivolous malpractice lawsuits also contribute to the myriad of problems facing our nation's health care system.

Health care delivery and the Medicare system are integral parts of our daily lives and of our economic infrastructure. Numerous problems exist in each, but, fortunately, we know how to solve the systemic challenges to efficient and affordable health care. Unfortunately, many members of our federal and state legislatures lack the necessary will and bold leadership to address the problems adequately. Many politicians feel that their chances for reelection are harmed with any mention of reducing government influence in health care.

The "new slavery," economic slavery, is more dangerous than the old slavery because you cannot see it in the public square or down on the plantation. As a result, it is tolerated through the generations because people feel there is little they can do to unshackle themselves from its grip on their lives. Economic slavery does not discriminate against one's race, sex, age, or religion. Those responsible for perpetuating economic slavery only care about one thing: controlling your life by controlling a growing amount of your money. Some of us may have arrived to this nation on the Mayflower, and some of us on slave ships, but we all are in the same boat now.

The City of Doubt—Washington, D.C.

All too often we read in the papers, see on television, or even hear in person a member of Congress bemoan the fact that it is just too difficult to advocate and enact fundamental policy change in Washington, D.C. The complaining members are, of course, always champions of policy change, but they just do not think they will be able to get the necessary support from their colleagues to tackle the big issues effectively.

Unfortunately, Washington, D.C. has become the "City of Doubt." Many of the would-be leaders in Washington campaign on promises of being able to fix problems, and then weeks after they are elected they are right back into politics as usual mode.

I believe the public is much more hopeful than members of Congress for the possibility of aggressive policy solutions. Veteran politicians have learned to campaign on hope and optimism, but then they go back to Washington and maintain "business as usual." They get away with maintaining the status quo because most voters turn off their political antennas the day after the election. Veteran politicians depend upon most voters having short memories or no memory at all.

If the majority of the electorate does not express a new voice after election day, the City of Doubt will never become a City of Hope. The City of Doubt will never replace the tax code mess or fix the broken Social Security structure. A City of Hope can fix these problems. We do not suffer from a deficiency of "know-how" in this country; we suffer from a deficiency of hope in Washington, D.C.

There are millions of success stories in every endeavor of life that prove we can accomplish anything when hope supersedes doubt. So why do most of our members of Congress campaign on hope and take doubt with them to Washington, D.C.? They either do not know how to lead or they lack the courage to lead.

Many professional politicians simply believe that if they do not take a bold leadership position on issues, their opponent in the next election will have no ammunition to use against them. Doing nothing is the politically safe option. Since the electoral process takes a long time to replace people, the public has got to push the elected officials that are in Congress now to do the right things and to do them with urgency.

Quite frankly, I am sick and tired of the status quo in D.C., and I believe millions of other voters feel the same way. We were founded as a nation of hope, not as a nation of doubt. Many of those we have elected have forgotten this principle.

The City of Doubt also refers to any city in our country where people have lost hope that it is possible to change the political status quo. The City of Doubt exists anywhere people have lost hope that it is possible for all citizens to work for and achieve economic freedom, and in any city, town, farm, or hollow where people have lost hope in their individual, God-given abilities to leave this great nation a little better than they found it for their children and grandchildren.

Tom Rath and the late Dr. Donald O. Clifton discuss the effects of lost hope in their book *How Full Is Your Bucket?* Rath and Clifton tell a heartbreaking story of the devastating and sometimes deadly effects of losing one's hope.

> Following the Korean War, Major (Dr.) William E. Mayer, who would later become the U.S. Army's chief psychiatrist, studied 1,000 American prisoners of war who had been detained in a North Korean camp. He was particularly interested in examining one of the most extreme and perversely effective cases of psychological warfare on record—one that had a devastating impact on its subjects.
>
> American soldiers had been detained in camps that were not considered especially cruel or unusual by conventional standards. The captive soldiers had adequate food, water, and shelter. They weren't subjected to common physical tactics of the time such as having bamboo shoots driven under their fingernails. In fact, fewer cases of physical abuse were reported in the North Korean POW camps than in prison camps from any other major military conflict throughout history.
>
> Why, then, did so many American soldiers die in these camps? They weren't hemmed in with barbed wire. Armed guards didn't surround the camps. Yet no soldier ever tried to escape. Furthermore, these men regularly broke rank and turned against each other, sometimes forming close relationships with their North Korean captors.

When the survivors were released to a Red Cross group in Japan, they were given the chance to phone loved ones to let them know they were alive. Very few bothered to make the call.

Upon returning home, the soldiers maintained no friendships or relationships with each other. Mayer described each man as being in a mental "solitary confinement cell . . . without any steel or concrete."

Mayer had discovered a new disease in the POW camps—a disease of extreme hopelessness. It was not uncommon for a soldier to wander into his hut and look despairingly about, deciding there was no use in trying to participate in his own survival. He would go into a corner alone, sit down, and pull a blanket over his head. And he would be dead within two days.

The soldiers actually called it "give up-itis." The doctors labeled it "marasmus," meaning, in Mayer's words, "a lack of resistance, a passivity." If the soldiers had been hit, spat upon, or slapped, they would have become angry. Their anger would have given them the motivation to survive. But in the absence of motivation, they simply died, even though there was no medical justification for their deaths.

Despite relatively minimal physical torture, "marasmus" raised the overall death rate in the North Korean POW camps to an incredible 38%—the highest POW death rate in U.S. military history. Even more astounding was that half of these soldiers died simply because they had given up. They had completely surrendered, both mentally and physically.

How could this have happened? The answers were found in the extreme mental tactics that the North Korean captors used. They employed what Mayer described as the "ultimate weapon" of war.

Mayer reported that the North Korean's objective was to "deny men the emotional support that comes from interpersonal relationships." To do this, the captors used four primary tactics: informing, self-criticism, breaking loyalty to leadership and country, and withholding all positive emotional support.

To encourage withholding, the North Koreans gave prisoners rewards such as cigarettes when they snitched on one another. But neither the offender nor the soldier reporting the violation was punished—the captors encouraged this practice for a different reason. Their intent was to break relationships and turn the men against each other.

To promote self-criticism, the captors gathered groups of 10 or 12 soldiers and employed what Mayer described as "a corruption of group psychotherapy." In these sessions, each man was required to stand up in front of the group and confess *all the bad things he had done*—as well as *all the good things he could have done but failed to do*. The most important part of this tactic was that the soldiers were not "confessing" to the North Koreans, but to their own peers.

The third major tactic that the captors employed was breaking loyalty to leadership and country. The primary way they did this was by slowly and relentlessly undermining a soldier's allegiance to his superiors. The consequences were ghastly.

In one case, a colonel instructed one of his men not to drink the water from a rice paddy field because he knew the organisms in the water might kill him. The soldier looked at his colonel and remarked, "Buddy, you ain't no colonel anymore; you're just a lousy prisoner like me. You take care of yourself, and I'll take care of me." The soldier died of dysentery a few days later.

If a soldier received a supportive letter from home, the captors withheld it. All negative letters, however—such as those telling of a relative passing away, or ones in which a wife wrote that she had given up on her husband's return as was going to remarry—were delivered to soldiers immediately.

The effects were devastating: The soldiers had nothing to live for and lost basic belief in themselves and their loved ones, not to mention God and country.

Excerpted from Tom Rath and Dr. Donald O. Clifton, *How Full Is Your Bucket?* (New York: Gallup Press, 2004), 17-23. Used by permission.

We can see from the experiences of some American POWs during the Korean War that, when taken to the extreme, the loss of hope can exert some of the most debilitating effects on our lives and the lives of our family members, and those we lead, work with or interact with on a regular basis.

Dr. Martin Luther King Jr. also noted the negative effects of a lack of hope in his famous and moving "I've Been to the Mountaintop" speech: "You know, whenever Pharaoh wanted to prolong the period of slavery in Egypt, he had a favorite, favorite formula for doing it . . . . He kept the slaves fighting among themselves."

Do political leaders in the U.S. utilize the tactics of Pharaoh or the North Koreans to create doubt in the minds of the public that enactment of aggressive policy solutions is ever possible? Of course they do. Democrats use these same tactics when they pit groups of U.S. citizens against each other with their divisive class warfare rhetoric instead of working on fixing our crumbling economic infrastructure.

They create doubt in people's minds that they can achieve economic freedom without assistance from a government program. They tell those in the so-called middle and lower economic classes that they are being kept down by the rich, and they tell Blacks that all their problems are caused by racist Whites. Democrats scare the elderly into thinking that Republicans want to cut their Social Security benefits or privatize the Social Security system.

They frame the issue of abortion around a woman's right to control her body against the men who want to control women's bodies. They have fought to take God out of our public schools, our courthouses, our Pledge of Allegiance, and have told school children they can no longer sing Christmas carols.

Democrats instill doubt in people's belief in their ability to achieve their American Dreams on an individual basis with individual responsibility. In doing so, they have helped create the politically homeless, who have given up on government and the prospect of change in the political status quo.

Some Republican leaders are also guilty of creating and perpetuating feelings of doubt among the public. Weeks after election day in 2004, a Republican senator, who is also chairman of a powerful committee, was asked about the prospect for replacing the tax code with a fairer system, given that Republicans now enjoyed an increased majority in the Senate. The senator stated, "Comprehensive tax reform would be difficult to do. I'm not one to spend a lot of time tilting at windmills." Instead of following the president's lead by working on a much needed replacement of the federal tax code, the senator chose to express doubt instead of hope for an aggressive solution to the tax code mess.

What would happen if your boss at work asked you on Monday to complete a task by Friday, and you said, "Boss, not only can that task not be completed by Friday, I don't think it can be completed at all. I'm not going to spend a lot of time tilting at your windmills." You would be on the unemployment line by Tuesday. You would be out of a job because, as an employee, your job is to answer to your boss. There is an expectation that you will complete the tasks you were hired to complete or you will be replaced by someone who is driven to excel and wants the company to succeed. We must hold our elected officials to results, or they will ride the wave of complacency.

All elected officials in the U.S. serve and are employed by the people who elect them. They are obligated to fix the problems of government and make the government operate as efficiently as possible. For too long, however, elected officials have preyed on a politically apathetic public. Instead of fixing our biggest problems, they have exacerbated them by annually spending billions on pork barrel projects for their home districts and heaping tax credit upon tax credit to the federal tax code mess with one objective in mind—do whatever it takes to keep the voters and campaign donors happy so they can get reelected.

It is no wonder why millions have lost hope in their government. Their government has forced them to lose hope in themselves, and their ability to be a new voice for policy change.

A Nation of Hope . . . We the People

Our nation has been blessed with many leaders in its history who faced seemingly insurmountable challenges and legions of doubters en route to achieving political victories that have forever changed the world. They have literally made possible what was once thought impossible. Leaders like Thomas Jefferson, Abraham Lincoln, John F. Kennedy, Dr. Martin Luther King Jr., and Ronald Reagan were not dissuaded by the doubters and political foes who told them their aspirations could not be achieved. Instead, they relied on their faith in God and the American people, their belief that anything can be accomplished in America, and their hope and optimism for the future.

Every day millions of Americans who possess those same qualities as our greatest political leaders carry with them the hope that today they too can get a little closer to making their American Dream a reality. I believe the majority of Americans are truly hopeful and optimistic people. In the face of the myriad of challenges we face each day, including, of course, those instilled by our political leaders, most Americans work hard every day to make their lives and the world a little better.

I believe that we are a nation of hope. Whether we will forever remain the *beacon* of hope for the world, however, depends on the willingness of the public to force our politicians to enact aggressive policies that will unleash our country's economic potential and protect our moral foundations. Solving problems and changing things begins with believing that it can be done, much like the bumblebee believes he can fly even though, mathematically, he is not supposed to fly.

Then how does the bumblebee fly? When I was a math major at Morehouse College, one of the things we studied was the equations of motion. The equations of motion are those equations that they put into computers to design airplanes and figure out how they are going to fly. Mathematicians and aerodynamicists for years have been trying to figure out mathematically and scientifically how the bumblebee flies. You see, the bumblebee is not supposed to fly. An aerodynamicist will tell you that the bumblebee's body is too big for its short little wings to suspend it in the air.

So the mathematicians and scientists take the aerodynamics of a bumblebee, of the little fat body and the little flappy wings, and put it all into a computer model. Then, they run the model with all of these measurements and the computer comes back and says, "The sucker can't fly." So out of frustration the next generation of mathematicians and aerodynamicists go get some more poor little bumblebees and put them in a wind tunnel. They take some more measurements. They get a bigger computer. They get a faster computer. They put it all in there, they run their models and equations, and the computer says, "The sucker still can't fly."

I'll tell you why the bumblebee flies. Nobody told the bumblebee that it could not fly. He just keeps flying around, gathering his nectar, and stinging you or your dog if you get too close. The bumblebee flies because he believes he can fly!

Like the bumblebee, we can change the status quo in government and can create a new brand identity for the party that represents the Government Of the People. We are a nation of hope because hope is the key to happiness, and happiness is the key to success. We have been successful as a nation because people have been free to define and pursue their own happiness. Self-motivation and happiness are synonymous because no one can make another person happy. If you are already happy you are motivated to stay happy, and if you are unhappy you have to be motivated to get happy. Many people have experienced the feeling of happiness without being able to explain or define the feeling. The same is also true of unhappiness.

A person who claims to be unhappy typically has a personal barrier to motivation. Happiness begins with a good attitude and with knowing what would really make you happy, but people cannot always answer that question.

A few years ago when I lived in Omaha I heard the minister of my church, Rev. Dr. Nigel McPherson, use some thought-provoking words to define happiness: "something to do, someone to love, and something to hope for." "Wow!" I thought to myself that Sunday morning when I first heard this definition. It makes so much sense and explains why I have felt a sense of happiness most of my life, although I did not know exactly why or how to articulate my sense of happiness.

I have always had something to do (school, work, career, more work, and even more work). I have always been blessed with loved ones (my parents, my wife, our children, and some very close friends). And I was never without hope for something . . . a healthy family, the next promotion, or the next adventure in my life or career.

But additionally, this definition gave me a vehicle to stir peoples' thinking who may be searching for happiness in their jobs and lives or who may be trying to eliminate a bad attitude.

If one of Reverend McPherson's "somethings" is missing, you have a happiness deficiency that only you can fill.

I believe much of the general public's dissatisfaction comes from an overload of negative news, negative political rhetoric, and the false perception that somehow the government or someone else is responsible for making them happy. This creates a mass bad attitude, which is a major barrier to happiness.

Something to do, someone to love, and something to hope for, but the greatest of these is hope. Hope has been the common thread of all the great leaders throughout the history of our nation. They have shared their hope and optimism for the future with their fellow citizens and inspired the public to believe in themselves and the possibility of positive change. There would be no great achievements in our history, and people would not be working hard to achieve their American Dreams, if it were not for hope.

Hope inspires people to believe in themselves and their abilities. Hope inspires people to start their own businesses or create the next great invention. Without hope in the prospect for success and a brighter future, we as individuals and as a nation are without purpose and vision. Hope is the basis for all achievements, great and small.

Hope inspired our Founding Fathers to declare their freedom from the tyranny of a distant king, and then fight and die to secure it for their children and the coming generations of freedom-seeking people from all over the world.

Hope inspired Thomas Jefferson to write in the Declaration of Independence,

> We hold these truths to be self-evident, that all men are created equal, that they are endowed by their Creator with certain unalienable Rights, that among these are Life, Liberty and the pursuit of Happiness . . . . . That whenever any Form of Government becomes destructive of these ends, it is the Right of the People

> to alter or to abolish it . . . . And for the support of
> this Declaration, with a firm reliance on the protec-
> tion of divine Providence, we mutually pledge to each
> other our Lives, our Fortunes and our sacred Honor.

With the stroke of a pen on July 4, 1776, fifty-six brave and hopeful colonists banded together and signed a document that set in motion the greatest experiment in history—the birth of the United States of America and a system of government by the people, of the people, and for the people.

Hope inspired President Abraham Lincoln to take all measures in his power to protect the Union during the tumultuous years of the Civil War. In his 1863 Gettysburg Address, he urged a public weary of war to continue the fight to preserve the Union and to remember all those who have come before to do the same:

> It is for us the living, rather, to be dedicated here to
> the unfinished work which they who fought here
> have thus far so nobly advanced. It is rather for us to
> be here dedicated to the great task remaining before
> us—that from these honored dead we take increased
> devotion to that cause for which they gave the last
> full measure of devotion—that we here highly resolve
> that these dead shall not have died in vain—that this
> nation, under God, shall have a new birth of
> freedom—and that government of the people, by the
> people, for the people, shall not perish from the
> earth.

Hope inspired President John F. Kennedy in his 1961 inaugural address to warn would-be aggressors that the United States stands ready to defend its freedoms and the freedoms of its allies across the world. In addition, he called on citizens to accept the responsibility of protecting America's freedoms,

Let every nation know, whether it wishes us well or
ill, that we shall pay any price, bear any burden, meet
any hardship, support any friend, oppose any foe to
assure the survival and the success of liberty.

In the long history of the world, only a few
generations have been granted the role of defending
freedom in its hour of maximum danger. I do not
shrink from this responsibility—I welcome it. I do
not believe that any of us would exchange places with
any other people or any other generation. The energy,
the faith, the devotion which we bring to this
endeavor will light our country and all who serve it—
and the glow from that fire can truly light the world.

And so, my fellow Americans: ask not what your
country can do for you—ask what you can do for
your country. My fellow citizens of the world: ask not
what America will do for you, but what together we
can do for the freedom of man.

Hope inspired Dr. Martin Luther King, Jr. to persist in the
great struggle for civil rights and equal opportunities for all
citizens, even when confronted by angry mobs, police beatings,
police dogs, fire hoses, jail sentences, and death threats. In his
1963 "I Have a Dream" speech, Dr. King inspired the entire
nation that in spite of all the obstacles he faced, his dream and
his persistence in seeing it come true had never faltered:

> We refuse to believe that there are insufficient funds
> in the great vaults of opportunity of this nation.
>
> Now is the time to rise from the dark and
> desolate valley of segregation to the sunlit path of
> racial justice. Now is the time to open the doors of
> opportunity to all of God's children. Now is the time
> to lift our nation from the quicksands of racial
> injustice to the solid rock of brotherhood.
>
> I say to you today, my friends, that in spite of the
> difficulties and frustrations of the moment, I still

have a dream. It is a dream deeply rooted in the American dream.

I have a dream that one day this nation will rise up and live out the true meaning of its creed: "We hold these truths to be self-evident: that all men are created equal."

With this faith we will be able to hew out of the mountain of despair a stone of hope.

Hope further inspired Dr. King at a rally on the night before he was assassinated to urge striking sanitation workers in Memphis to remain steadfast in their struggle:

Let us rise up tonight with a greater readiness. Let us stand with a greater determination.

And let us move on in these powerful days, these days of challenge to make America what it ought to be. We have an opportunity to make America a better nation.

I just want to do God's will. And He's allowed me to go up to the mountain. And I've looked over. And I've seen the Promised Land. I may not get there with you. But I want you to know tonight, that we, as a people, will get to the Promised Land!

Hope inspired President Ronald Reagan on many occasions. President Reagan was one of the most hopeful, optimistic leaders in the history of the United States. His belief in the spirit and abilities of the American people and peoples throughout the world was unwavering, and his faith in God and belief that He has a special purpose for our country resolute. In his 1981 Inaugural Speech, Reagan stated,

We hear much of special interest groups. Well, our concern must be for a special interest group that has been too long neglected. It knows no sectional boundaries, or ethnic and racial divisions, and it crosses political party lines. It is made up of men and women who raise our food, patrol our streets, man our mines and factories, teach our children, keep our homes, and heal us when we're sick—professionals, industrialists, shopkeepers, clerks, cabbies, and truck drivers. They are, in short, "We the People." This breed called Americans. . . . The crisis we are facing today does not require of us the kind of sacrifice that . . . so many thousands of others were called upon to make. It does require, however, our best effort, and our willingness to believe in ourselves and to believe in our capacity to perform great deeds; to believe that together with God's help we can and will resolve the problems that now confront us. And after all, why shouldn't we believe that? We are Americans.

Reagan's hope and optimism in a 1987 speech in front of the Berlin Wall inspired the world that communism could be defeated and freedoms made available to all people who seek them: "General Secretary Gorbachev, if you seek peace, if you seek prosperity for the Soviet Union and Eastern Europe, if you seek liberalization: Come here to this gate! Mr. Gorbachev, open this gate! Mr. Gorbachev, tear down this wall! Yes, across Europe, this wall will fall. For it cannot withstand faith; it cannot withstand truth. The wall cannot withstand freedom."

A number of common themes permeate the words of Jefferson, Lincoln, Kennedy, King, and Reagan. Among these are an enduring faith in God and an understanding that He created our great nation and all its promises and has charged its citizens with its protection.

President George W. Bush referenced this charge in a speech I heard him give in 2004 when he stated, "Democracy is not America's gift to the world, it is God's gift to the world, and our responsibility to protect it."

A second common theme is that these great men understood America's unique place in the world. We are not a conquering nation, but we will fight to the end against those who wish to bring us harm. We are a nation of individuals in pursuit of our individual dreams, but we are bound together by a love for the freedoms necessary to allow us to pursue our dreams and aspirations.

The third common theme in the words and lives of these great leaders is hope and optimism. Each one overcame extraordinary obstacles to achieve extraordinary goals. They were not always successful in each step along the path to success, but their hope and optimism allowed them to persevere and achieve their "calling." Hope and optimism allowed each one of these leaders to change the country and the world forever.

Dr. Robert Schuller calls this hope and optimism "possibility thinking." The late Don Clifton describes it as "positive psychology." The Apostle Paul calls it "faith." I call it "the key to happiness."

Perhaps the most important lesson to be learned from the lives and words of Jefferson, Lincoln, Kennedy, King, and Reagan is that there will always be a greater number of people around us who are consumed by doubt and defeatism who, for various reasons, want to stop us at all costs from accomplishing our goals. And yet, the most successful among us, those of us who will achieve the greatest successes, dream the biggest dreams and make them all come true, are those of us consumed by hope and optimism.

Those of us who are not afraid to challenge the status quo in Washington will be the ones responsible for forcing Congress to enact aggressive policy change. Those who demonstrate the initiative to start their own grassroots movement, grow that movement, and show members of Congress that their political futures rest on changing the status quo and on leading the nation out of problems instead of watching problems get worse.

This great nation was built on the shoulders of those filled with hope and those who believed in a better tomorrow despite the obstacles. We *can* force Congress to unshackle us from the chains of economic slavery and allow all citizens the opportunity to achieve economic freedom. As our nation's forefathers have shown us, it all begins with faith, optimism, and hope.

SUMMARY FOR CHAPTER 5

We Are *All* in the Same Boat Now

- The terrorist attacks on September 11, 2001, reminded us that we are a nation of individuals who share many of the same hopes and dreams.
- In a crisis we unite. In times of prolonged prosperity we fight among ourselves like cats and dogs. Terrorism is a crisis. The war against our economic foundations is a crisis.

Terrorists Want to Kill All of Us

- Support of our president and our military should not be partisan as they prosecute the war on terrorism. Otherwise, the terrorists will be victorious in their mission to instill fear, divide, and destroy our great nation.
- Democrats and the liberal media must not be allowed to plant the seeds of doubt that destroy hope in our abilities, weaken the morale of the public and military personnel, and divide rather than unite us.

Economic Slavery for All

- The "new slavery" is not the slavery of one man owning another as his property, but *economic slavery*—slavery to a tax code and Social Security system that are out of control.
- The federal tax code, Social Security, and Medicare, enacted in 1913, 1935, and 1965, respectively, are the three pillars that support our nation's economic infrastructure. All three systems are in a mess and have been for decades.
- The federal income tax code must be replaced. Several commissions over the last twenty years have all concluded

that a replacement tax system should satisfy six criteria. The FairTax (a national sales tax) satisfies *all* six criteria.

- The Social Security system is nearing bankruptcy due to decades of mismanagement, a flawed structure, and a lack of leadership and the political will in Congress for meaningful change. It must be replaced by a system of personal retirement investment.

- The health care system in the United States is severely sick. It is unduly influenced by the federal government, federal regulatory agencies, state governments, state regulatory agencies, insurance companies, and trial lawyers.

- Some of us may have arrived to this nation on the Mayflower, and some of us on slave ships, but we all are in the same boat now.

The City of Doubt—Washington, D.C.

- The public is much more hopeful than members of Congress for the possibility of aggressive policy solutions. Veteran politicians have learned to campaign on hope and optimism, but then they go back to Washington and maintain business as usual.

- Most voters turn off their political antennas the day after the election. Veteran politicians depend upon most voters having short memories or no memory at all.

- It is no wonder why millions have lost hope in their government. Their government has forced them to lose hope in themselves and their ability to be a new voice for policy change. If the majority of the electorate does not express a new voice after election day, the City of Doubt will never become a City of Hope.

A Nation of Hope . . . We the People

- Our nation has been blessed with many leaders in its history who faced seemingly insurmountable challenges and legions of doubters en route to achieving political victories that have forever changed the world.

- Leaders like Thomas Jefferson, Abraham Lincoln, John F. Kennedy, Dr. Martin Luther King Jr., and Ronald Reagan were not dissuaded by the doubters. A number of common themes permeate the words of these great leaders, including an enduring faith in God, an understanding of America's unique place in the world, and a sense of hope and optimism.
- We can force Congress to unshackle us from the chains of economic slavery and allow all citizens the opportunity to achieve economic freedom. As our nation's forefathers have shown us, it all begins with faith, optimism, and hope.

A New Model to Inspire Voters

A New Voice

There is an old wives' tale that says if you put a frog in a pot of boiling water, it will jump out. But if you put a frog in a pot of cold water and add just a little bit of heat, the frog will adjust to the change and stay there. Then you add another little bit of heat, and the frog will adjust again. If you continue to add a little bit of heat over a long period of time, the frog will eventually boil to death without even realizing it.

Like the frog in that tale, the public has been conditioned since the enactment of our tax code (1913), Social Security system (1935), and Medicare program (1965) to accept incremental losses of our individual economic freedoms. Congress has gradually taken more and more of our money, and with it our economic freedom, through numerous forms of taxation to fund the federal government's entitlement programs and pork barrel spending. We the people have allowed it to happen.

When our Founding Fathers boldly declared "life, liberty, and the pursuit of happiness" as the foundation of what has become the greatest nation in the world, they also required us to "alter or abolish any form of government" which becomes destructive of those ideals. The tax code mess, the Social Security mess, and the Medicare mess are destroying those ideals *and* our economic freedom.

Our form of government was designed with a system of checks and balances to help ensure sound public policy. On the other hand, the system makes it difficult to change public policy quickly unless there is a crisis. Whenever there is a threat to our national security the president and Congress have historically reacted with a heightened sense of urgency. The attack on our economic security has been a slow boil, but most people do not yet feel the heat.

The inefficiency and unfairness of the tax code and the coming train wrecks for Social Security and Medicare are well documented. But the collective sense of urgency of the president, Congress, *and* the public has been absent. The general public has become conditioned to expect minimal changes from Congress, and Congress has perpetuated that expectation. As a result, our nation faces a growing list of other important problems, which are compounded by the new and different war on terrorism. But if we do not stop the gradual collapse of our economic infrastructure, the list of other important issues will become irrelevant.

News and information overload has produced a society of incomplete information, unclear thought, and uncertain feelings about nearly all political issues and events. We have been bombarded with too many sound bites, not enough information, and too few facts. People's lives are crammed with too many things to do in the same twenty-four-hour day. As a result, many people are making critical decisions based on isolated factoids of data, which are often not any better than the flip of a coin.

This is why we have constant gridlock in Congress, more too-close-to-call elections, confusing public opinion polls, unsolved decades-old national problems, a declining moral conscience, and a growing lack of personal responsibility. The future of this nation will be determined by the degree to which the general public can better connect the headlines of the day to the facts and their lives and the degree to which government can accelerate its ability to address the big issues effectively. A new model of government is not required to fix these problems, but a new sense of urgency is long overdue.

This nation is richly blessed with *know-how*, but a deficiency of *right-now*. Solving the big problems is not a matter of having the *skill* to solve them. It is a matter of having the *will* to solve them. In order for aggressive solutions to rise to the top of the public's mind-set and the forefront of congressional action, we must systematically and consistently challenge the status quo with a passion for change, or we will continue to get more of the same. We must demand greater urgency from our elected leaders in Congress, and we must demand more intelligent participation from the general public.

Technology has dramatically transformed our nation and our lives and continues to do so at an accelerated rate. We must change public policy at an accelerated rate on the big three critical systems to create a new day in government and a new day in the economic lives of working citizens. To accomplish this will require *A New Voice*.

A New Voice is the voice of those voters who are tired of politics and politicians as usual. It is a voice of common sense and urgency. It is the voice of aggressive solutions to solve our nations' most pressing economic issues and to liberate working people from what has become economic slavery.

A New Voice is not a political party; it's a purpose. That purpose is to inform, educate, and inspire motivated voters to leverage their collective voices to bring about more aggressive congressional action on the big issues.

A *New Voice* believes that our government can work the way our Founding Fathers intended.

Our strategy is simple. Stay focused on a few big issues. Establish a highly motivated and mobilized base of voters. Make our voices heard in Congress clearly, swiftly, and consistently.

We will execute this strategy by maximizing the use of technology, establishing an interconnected network of voters, and maximizing media exposure to produce a new model for impacting public policy.

Soon, the politically homeless will have a home.

Maximizing Technology

In 1971 while studying for my Master's degree in computer science, one of the ongoing academic debates was about the future of centralized versus distributed computer processing. IBM was the largest computer company in the world and led in the manufacture and sale of large mainframe computers. It was not unusual for businesses and organizations to have large rooms filled with their "big boxes," as they were sometimes called.

Those who argued on behalf of more and more centralized processing were proved dead wrong. Computer processing power is everywhere now! Sometimes it is abused, but it is everywhere. We can see examples of computer technology every day, from our desktop computer to the car we drive to our cell phone. A typical cell phone has as much or more computer processing power than a typical big box mainframe of the 1970s.

Laptop and desktop computers are everywhere, and let's not forget the latest handheld combination phone and computer that fits in your pocket and is no bigger than a typical cell phone. I resisted getting one of these devices when I was running for the U.S. Senate but finally gave in to my staff's insistence and found it indispensable. I had to learn how to type with my thumbs, but I have gotten pretty good at it.

We are a technologically, 24/7, connected society. When you add snail-mail, e-mail, direct mail, junk mail, and incessant media madness on top of it all, it is easy to understand why many people suffer from information overload. In many cases, it is incomplete or misleading information overload. We are all exposed to more and more stuff, faster and faster, and it all started with the microchip.

Successful businesses have learned how to maximize technology in order to remain competitive. Government agencies have tried to keep up for the sake of improved efficiencies with the people's money. Political campaigns maximize their resources using technology to better target voters. Associations and advocacy organizations have embraced technology for communicating with their constituencies and releasing an avalanche of influence on Congress at strategic opportunities.

Helping to get candidates elected with views and opinions consistent with one's constituency is no longer enough to impact public policy. Effective follow-up between elections is also required using advances in technology, due to the plethora of political forces pulling on a senator or representative after they are elected. Election day is not the end of voter influence over the legislative process. It's the beginning, because too many veteran politicians campaign on hope and enthusiasm, then return to the status quo and doubt when they get reelected.

A New Voice is your voice. It will maximize technology through the usual and some not-so-usual means to keep its voices engaged and inspired after election day. While many organizations have struggled to keep up with technology, *a New Voice* will maximize technology to develop a Vocal, Interconnected, and Persistent (VIP) network of voters.

VIP Network

The information highway is loaded with reckless drivers. We cannot believe everything we see and hear on the Internet, and the trust many of us once put in the major television networks' newscasts was shaken during the 2004 election cycle with numerous examples of deliberately biased reporting and forged documents. *A New Voice* will counteract these reckless drivers with compelling facts, completed stories, and common sense observations. With these message characteristics and by focusing on a few big issues, *A New Voice* will be heard above the clutter more often with its VIP network.

During the 2004 presidential election, Senator John Kerry and Democratic candidates repeatedly called the U.S. economy failed or lousy because of President Bush's economic policies. They were repeatedly wrong! Using research compiled by the Media Research Center (MRC), one could easily observe that their campaign rhetoric did not match the facts of the economic situation.

Here are the *facts*. The following table provides a comparison of metrics for the economy during the 1996 reelection year for President Bill Clinton versus the economic metrics in 2004 during President Bush's reelection race.

Comparison of the Metrics on U.S. Economy, 1996 and 2004		
Economic Indicator	**Clinton 1996**	**Bush 2004**
Unemployment	5.2%	5.4%
Gross Domestic Product Growth	2.2%	4.5%
Inflation	3.0%	2.7%
Continuous Months of Positive Job Growth	7	12j

Source: Media Research Center

As mentioned previously, the MRC research report show that news stories about the 1996 economy under President Clinton were positive 85 percent of the time. News stories about the 2004 economy under President Bush were positive only 13 percent of the time. Maybe there is something to this liberal media bias conspiracy theory.

I had several opportunities to debate Democrat officials or candidates during the 2004 presidential campaign on television and radio programs and I shared with them these compelling facts. They were not interested in the facts. They persistently stayed with the Democrat script of bash, distort, and smear. To paraphrase Jack Nicholson's character in the movie *A Few Good Men*, "They can't handle the *facts!*"

I was only one new voice of a few people aware of these facts. Just think of the impact when we have millions of new voices to counter all the junk scattered on the information highway.

Examples of incomplete stories can be seen all the time in newspapers and heard on television and radio news programs. Most incomplete stories are "sound bite" driven, and the media usually tries to personalize the stories by describing their version of a typical person or family, which was selected more for emotional appeal than any statistically representative situation.

Consider this example in the following table:

Article: "Suburbs' grass isn't always greener"
Date: 10/18/04
Media: USA Today

The Story:

(1) For the first time, the number of poor people in the suburbs almost equals the number in cities at the center of metropolitan areas.

(2) Immigration, the dispersal of people who lived in urban housing projects that have been torn down, and revitalization of blighted neighborhoods by the affluent are cited as factors that "export" those in poverty to suburban areas.

(3) Profile of two families:
  • Divorced mother, college graduate, mother of two, makes $5.15/hour
  • Family of five making $50,000/year

What the Headlines Don't Tell You:

(1) The definition of "suburb" is not the same as it was 50 or maybe even 20 years ago. Increased housing construction at nearly all price levels in areas outside metropolitan areas means that, technically, a "suburb" exists for all income levels.

(2) This article does not discuss the fact that all those people studied have children they cannot pay for. Having children is not a right – it is a privilege and a responsibility.

(3) Prices on everything have soared in 20 years, including housing. However, interest rates are at all time lows, which have allowed more people to purchase their first home. Not necessarily their BEST home, but their FIRST home.

(4) Income taxes increased in 1993 under President Clinton. Personal savings per U.S. family have decreased ever since from over 7% per household to less than 1%.

Common sense Observations:

(1) Poverty in suburbs is rising due to costs <u>and</u> cost of government.

(2) Personal responsibility and individual choices greatly affect one's opportunities for financial achievement.

(3) Change the way people pay taxes; namely, on what they **spend**, not on what they earn (the FairTax).

Compelling facts, completed stories, and common sense observations by millions of new voices are a powerful weapon against what Brent Bozell, President of the MRC, calls the "weapons of mass distortion."

Your vocal, interconnected, and persistent involvement in influencing public policy is the key to growing *A New Voice*, expanding your own VIP network, and saving our economic infrastructure. As a self-motivated new voice, there are no limits to your ability to influence others on the urgency for aggressive policy solutions!

You can begin your own involvement in saving our economic infrastructure by first contacting those in your existing networks of influence. This includes your friends and family members, people in your e-mail distribution list, members of your place of worship, members of your neighborhood association, loved ones on your holiday card list, and members of your community, civic, or service organization. These are the people who know, respect, and trust you.

Send an issue awareness or issue endorsement letter or e-mail to members of your networks. The letter introduces those in your networks to the issue, urges them to support it and provides supporting reasons, and urges them to contact their own networks of influence.

Contact your U.S. representative and senators and ask them to support replacing the tax code, restructuring Social Security, and removing government interference in Medicare and our health care system. Urge your legislators to become leaders in Congress in passing legislation related to each issue.

You can also spread the message of economic freedom through local and national media outlets. Write a letter to the editor of your local newspaper that states your support for a particular issue. Call local and nationally syndicated talk radio programs and discuss the issues and the urgent need to enact aggressive policy solutions. Share your views on the issues on Internet discussion groups and blogs.

Solutions to our big issues are lost in denial, empty rhetoric, misrepresentations, bureaucracy, and personal agendas. In order for real solutions to rise to the top of the public's mind-set and the forefront of congressional action, we must consistently challenge the status quo and elect senators and representatives who share our passion for change. Take every opportunity available to volunteer your time for candidates who are truly committed to challenging the status quo in Congress. The following table illustrates the many opportunities you have to become *A New Voice* and influence public policy decisions.

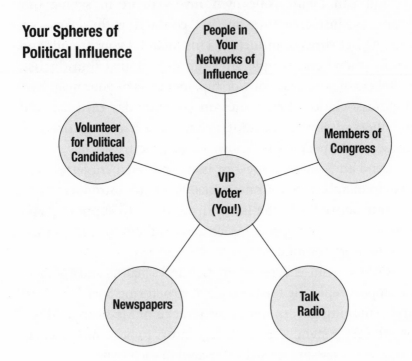

Maximizing Media Exposure

There's an old saying, "Fight fire with fire." The often incomplete reporting and liberal bias of mainstream media is well documented. Although Brent Bozell and the MRC do a great job of keeping many media outlets' and producers' feet to the fire, it is a never-ending battle. There are newspapers, magazines, newsletters, television and radio programs, and Internet sites that regularly present the conservative side of many issues, but the daily battle against the liberal media establishment is similar to David's fight against Goliath. The good news is that the conservative David is growing, and he did defeat Goliath in the end.

A New Voice will capitalize on numerous media opportunities to promote its messages of aggressive solutions and economic liberation of working people. My 2004 U.S. Senate campaign demonstrated that there are hundreds of thousands of people who have an appetite for challenging the status quo in order to fix the big problems. Members of Congress and the media will pay attention when millions of politically homeless across the country begin to make their voices heard.

A New Voice has a unique personality with a multidimensional background to lead this unique endeavor: "The Hermanator." Here's how Larry McCarthy of Gannon, McCarthy & Mason, Ltd., describes the origin of "The Hermanator":

> Around the time we were working with Herman Cain on health care reform and other National Restaurant Association issues in 1994, I stumbled across the movie *The Terminator* while cable grazing.
>
> One of my favorite lines from the movie is Arnold Schwarzenegger's guttural catch phrase "I'll be back," an especially appropriate line for a character who was impossible to stop and kept popping up everywhere.
>
> At the time, Herman was receiving very heavy press coverage for his "debate" with President Clinton on health care and appearing all over the country on a variety of issues. Herman was impossible to stop and kept popping up everywhere. Hence, "The Hermanator."

The new voices will not go it alone on our mission to save our economic foundations. There are dozens of organizations that are our strategic partners in this new vision, and many have been fighting the good fight for many years.

The mission of *A New Voice* is to leverage its members and those of its strategic alliances into a more focused and inspired VIP network. It is not the intent of *A New Voice* to reinvent the wheel; our objective is to connect the spokes of the wheel so common sense can conquer insanity.

The need for *A New Voice* that utilizes cutting edge technology and a VIP network to influence public policy and tell the truth about issues and the best solutions is long overdue. Major media outlets do not help us. Our elected officials get timid about aggressive policy solutions. And most of the general public is apathetic and absent. Granted, there are many associations and organizations working to protect the issues of their respective constituencies, but the issues of *A New Voice* transcend industry, political party, race, sex, or income level.

Our collective task is to create a VIP network of voices capable of dramatically influencing what goes on in Washington, D.C. between elections. Congress has repeatedly demonstrated that it does not act without public pressure applied heavily and frequently.

Fortunately, President Bush has demonstrated that he is not afraid to lead. In fact, during his Economic Summit in December 2004, he stated, "I came to Washington to solve problems." With majorities of Republicans in both the House and the Senate, I believe he will do just that, if Congress will follow. Our job is to make sure that they do indeed follow. Otherwise, in the next election our job will be to make sure they get out of the way.

A New Nation

Most people do not object to providing assistance to their fellow citizens either directly or by way of efficient government assistance programs, but no one is entitled to the fruits of another man's labor. Our current methods of taxation and redistribution of income follow the foolish directive of Karl Marx: *From each according to his abilities, to each according to his needs.* Our so-called progressive system of taxation at the federal level is based on the premise that those who make the highest incomes should pay proportionately the most for the government services that benefit all citizens.

Those at the lowest income levels are in fact hit the hardest by our system of taxation. One hundred percent of their wages are subject to the Social Security and Medicare taxes, which are of course automatically withheld from their paychecks. When they retire and begin receiving their monthly Social Security benefits, they are taxed again because our government considers your Social Security benefits income—*even though you already earned the money decades ago!*

Contrary to the thinking of many members of Congress, our systems of taxation and income redistribution are inherently unfair to every citizen because they do not treat every citizen equally. Additionally, the "more you earn the more you pay" principle is a bigger disincentive to the low wage earner than to the high wage earner. Why? Because just as it takes more fuel to accelerate a car to cruising speed than it does to maintain cruising speed, a worker has to work harder and earn more proportionately to get into economic cruise control. As a result, many people never get there.

Our current economic infrastructure, the tax code and Social Security system, punishes everybody because of progressive tax rates on what people earn and massive government inefficiency.

Our elected leaders in Congress insult our intelligence every day. They simply do not think we are capable of managing our own money, of saving and investing in our own futures. Many in Congress obviously have the desire to create a socialist system that adheres to Karl Marx's vision. They just have not been honest enough to say it out loud.

What would Thomas Jefferson, author of our Declaration of Independence and one of the preeminent political minds in history, think of our current taxation policies and entitlement and discretionary federal spending that exceeds the entire GDP of many nations? Listen to Jefferson's words on these issues.

Thomas Jefferson on taxation:

> The taxes with which we are familiar class [classify)] themselves readily according to the basis on which they rest: 1. Capital. 2. Income. 3. Consumption . . . . A government may select either of these bases for the establishment of its system of taxation, and so frame it as to reach the faculties of every member of the society, and to draw from him his equal proportion of the public contributions . . . . But when once a government has assumed its basis, to select and tax special articles from either of the other classes, is double taxation . . . . For that portion of Income with which these articles are purchased, having already paid its tax as Income, to pay another tax on the thing it purchased, is paying twice for the same thing; it is an aggrievance on the citizens who use these articles in exoneration of those who do not, contrary to the most sacred of the duties of a government, to do equal and impartial justice to all its citizens.

Our government is clearly not providing "equal and impartial justice to all its citizens." Every citizen who earns a wage is taxed on his or her income, but we are also taxed again when that income is invested and grows—what the tax code calls a "capital gain." We are also all subject to local taxes on consumption—sales taxes—when we purchase retail goods. Our money, therefore, is "triple-taxed." And when we die, we are taxed again!

Thomas Jefferson on excessive federal spending:

> I do not know on what principles of reasoning it is that good men think the public ought to pay more for a thing than they would themselves if they wanted it. (1808)
>
> To preserve the faith of the nation by an exact discharge of its debts and contracts, expend the public money with the same care and economy we would practice with our own, and impose on our citizens no unnecessary burden ... are the landmarks by which we are to guide ourselves in all our proceedings. (1802)

Congress is losing the faith of the nation because it does not adhere to our Founders' warnings to spend within our means, and it unnecessarily burdens current and future generations with needless debt. There are certainly times in our history when it is necessary to incur budget deficits. For example, we are currently engaged in a war against terrorists to protect our borders and our freedoms. Congress is justified in spending the amounts needed to equip our military personnel and secure our borders.

The public loses faith in the ability of Congress to sensibly and honestly control the nation's purse strings, however, when it approves 50 million dollars to construct an indoor rainforest in Iowa, 15 million for dairy development programs overseas through the U.S. Agency for International Development, and 13 million for United Nations programs. These are just three of the thousands of pork barrel spending projects that cost U.S. taxpayers billions of dollars each year.

Surely Thomas Jefferson had in mind greater ideals for Congress and a greater vision of freedom for American citizens when he stated, in 1826,

> May [our Declaration of Independence] be to the
> world, what I believe it will be (to some parts sooner,
> to others later, but finally to all), the signal of
> arousing men to burst the chains under which
> monkish ignorance and superstition had persuaded
> them to bind themselves, and to assume the blessings
> and security of self-government . . . . All eyes are
> opened, or opening, to the rights of man.

We must demand that Congress end the usurpation of our
rights and freedoms. If we do not urgently demand greater
accountability from Congress, our children and grandchildren
will live under a system of government more oppressive than
that from which Thomas Jefferson and the Founding Fathers
declared their independence.

Dr. Martin Luther King, Jr. showed millions of people of all
races that it is possible to achieve equal rights and opportunities
through nonviolent protest. Dr. King reminded this nation that
all our citizens must be allowed access to "life, liberty, and the
pursuit of happiness," and that we are all God's children, regardless of our skin color. What would Dr. King think of today's
Democratic Party, the party that fought so hard against his
mission but eventually became the political home to the vast
majority of Black voters?

Since his death in 1968, the Democratic Party and some of
Dr. King's followers have used the King name to create their own
legacies through hateful rhetoric, divisive political policies, and
even corruption and scandal. Jesse Jackson, Julian Bond, and
Joseph Lowery all stood behind Dr. King throughout his
struggle to achieve the great civil rights victories of the 1950s
and 1960s, but since his death they have abandoned his dreams
and the principles he expressed. In their own struggles to
remain relevant participants in the national political process,
these so-called Black leaders have worked hard to convince
generations of Blacks that it is because of their race that they

cannot achieve in school and business, and that the days of suffering and segregation are still upon us but in slightly different forms.

I believe Dr. King would be appalled at the pessimism some of his followers have instilled in tens of millions of Blacks. He would be appalled that instead of conveying a new dream to the next generation of Black voters, the dream of economic freedom and self-determination, these self-appointed leaders are mired in the self-serving business of keeping all Blacks on the Democrat plantation.

When Dr. King said, "Now is the time to open the doors of opportunity to all of God's children," he meant more than just the doors of segregation and voting rights. Dr. King knew that no citizen, regardless of race, is truly free to access life, liberty, and the pursuit of happiness until they have the opportunity to pursue economic freedom.

In his speech titled "I've Been to the Mountaintop" Dr. King said, "Let us rise up tonight with a greater readiness. Let us stand with a greater determination. And let us move on in these powerful days, these days of challenge to make America what it ought to be. We have an opportunity to make America a better nation." With these ringing words of inspiration Dr. King challenged all Americans to believe in themselves and their abilities to determine their own futures. I believe he would be disappointed in the actions and rhetoric some of his followers and the Democratic Party have employed to discourage, not inspire, Blacks from achieving educational and economic success through their own self-determination.

Dr. King understood that it is the issues that are important, not which party pays lip service to them. That is why Dr. King, Ralph Abernathy, and former Atlanta mayor and U.S. Ambassador Andrew Young supported President Eisenhower's 1956 reelection campaign. President Eisenhower supported positive civil rights legislation and appointed federal judges who protected the civil rights of all citizens.

Dr. King would not want Blacks beholden to a political party simply for the sake of tradition, especially when that party supports policies that hinder Blacks' prospects for educational and economic success. I believe today Dr. King would tell his followers and the Democratic Party, "Our issues transcend politics. You can no longer take our votes for granted; they now come with a price, and that price is called accountability." As Ambassador Young told me during my own campaign, "We do not have a permanent party—we have permanent issues."

The Reagan Revolution of the 1980s occurred when millions of inspired citizens, including many former Democratic voters, were reenergized about their possibilities to achieve economic freedom and their American Dreams. Through his words and policies President Ronald Reagan gave his country inspired hope and opportunity. President Reagan was himself a former Democrat who saw that party's leaders grow the power and influence of the federal government and rob the nation of its collective spirit and belief in individual achievement through hard work and self-determination.

President Reagan understood that our nation's greatness comes from its citizens, not from politicians and bureaucrats squirreled away in Washington, D.C. He knew that to change the policies of the past he would have to inspire the people to make their voices heard. Reagan's passion and policies reinvigorated the American entrepreneurial spirit, produced economic freedom for millions, and showed a new generation that conservative fiscal policies and smaller federal government can provide the greatest opportunity for economic success.

What would President Reagan think of today's Republican Party, which seems to have lost the hope for changing the status quo in Washington through aggressive policy solutions? President Reagan did not have the luxury of Republican majorities in both houses of Congress. Through his leadership and ability to communicate his message directly to the people, however, he showed that change in the status quo was possible.

Like President Reagan before him, President George W. Bush believes that for people to control their own destinies and achieve their dreams they must have the opportunity to control "the fruits of their labor." President Bush shares Reagan's faith in God and in the American people and, better yet, has a Congress controlled by fellow Republicans. President Bush has demonstrated a passion for change and an ability to lead on enacting solutions to the big issues.

Congressional Republicans, however, are not unified behind their current president. Many of today's congressional Republicans are mired in the doubt that change is possible. They are too wrapped up in the politics of politics and protecting their own sandboxes. They are too concerned with their own political careers and not the economic futures they will leave our children and our grandchildren. Instead of a twenty-first-century vision of securing and protecting our economic infrastructure, they have a two- or six-year vision of securing their reelection.

I believe President Reagan would be disappointed that many of today's Republican leaders, many of whom became involved in the political arena because of Reagan's inspiration, have decided to place themselves before policy solutions. He would question their reasons for publicly questioning the need for aggressive policy changes. President Reagan did not view aggressive tax policy changes as "tilting at windmills," as a senior senator expressed. President Reagan correctly saw these aggressive changes as required policy to save our country from long-term economic misery.

Today's congressional Republicans, from the leaders to the rank-and-file, must summon the courage and passion of President Reagan, Dr. King, John F. Kennedy, and Abraham Lincoln to believe that aggressive change is possible. They must then have the courage and provide the leadership necessary to restore the economic freedom we once had. President Bush cannot do it all by himself. He has chosen to lead aggressively, but he needs the assistance of those in his party who must place the interests of the nation before their own political careers.

President Reagan knew that we are blessed with only a scarce few opportunities to succeed and achieve our dreams in whatever endeavors we pursue. Our nation is now blessed with one of those rare opportunities to secure our economic foundations for future generations. Congressional Republicans must not squander the opportunity.

This is a unique opportunity to restore the "new nation" Abraham Lincoln referred to in his address at Gettysburg in 1863: "Four score and seven years ago our fathers brought forth upon this continent a new nation, conceived in liberty, and dedicated to the proposition that all men are created equal." This is a unique opportunity to inspire that "fierce urgency of now" that Dr. King talked about while speaking in Washington, D.C. in 1963: "We have also come to this hallowed spot to remind America of the fierce urgency of now. This is no time to engage in the luxury of cooling off or to take the tranquilizing drug of gradualism."

We have put the names of Jefferson, Lincoln, Kennedy, King, Reagan, and many of our other founders and greatest leaders on schools, streets, federal buildings, our money, and even declared holidays in their honor. Are those actions enough to truly honor their lives? *No*! In addition to the schools and buildings and streets we must also honor their lives by meeting and exceeding the ideals they fought and, at times, died for.

Our greatest act to honor their memories and preserve their shared vision is never to end the struggle to achieve their shared beliefs in self-government, accountability to the people, economic freedom for all citizens, faith in the spirit of the American people, and faith in God. Above all else, we must never allow a nation built on hope and optimism to lose its ability to dream and to achieve great things.

SUMMARY FOR CHAPTER 6

A New Model to Inspire Voters

A New Voice

- When our Founding Fathers boldly declared "life, liberty, and the pursuit of happiness" as the foundation of what has become the greatest nation in the world, they also required us to "alter or abolish any form of government" that becomes destructive of those ideals.

- *A New Voice* is the voice of those voters who are tired of politics and politicians as usual. It is a voice of common sense and urgency. It is the voice of aggressive solutions to solve our nations' most pressing economic issues and to liberate working people from what has become economic slavery.

- *A New Voice* is not a political party; it's a purpose. That purpose is to inform, educate, and inspire self-motivated voters to leverage their collective voices to bring about more aggressive congressional action on the "big" issues.

- The strategy of *A New Voice* is simple. Stay focused on a few big issues. Establish a highly self-motivated and mobilized base of voters. Make our voices heard in Congress clearly, swiftly, and consistently.

- The mission of *A New Voice* is to leverage its members and those of its strategic alliances into a more focused and inspired grassroots movement.

A New Nation

- Most people do not object to providing assistance to their fellow citizens either directly or by way of efficient government assistance programs, but no one is entitled to the fruits of another man's labor.

- Our current economic infrastructure, the tax code and Social Security system, punishes everybody because of progressive tax rates on what people earn and massive government inefficiency.
- Our nation is now blessed with one of those rare opportunities to secure our economic foundations for future generations. Congressional Republicans must not squander the opportunity.
- Our greatest act to honor their (Lincoln, King, and Reagan) memories and preserve their shared vision is never to end the struggle to achieve their shared beliefs in self-government, accountability to the people, economic freedom for all citizens, faith in the spirit of the American people, and faith in God.

Chapter 7

My Inspired Journey

If you do not believe in God, you will not believe this chapter. I believe that my decision to run for the U.S. Senate, which subsequently led to writing this book and now the next phase of my life's journey, was divinely inspired. Indeed, this has been the case for every major career decision I have made in my life. Being on a God-inspired fast track of success and surviving the many things that could have gone wrong was no accident.

The concept of having a dream or "decade goal" for each decade of my life was also God-inspired, because most twenty-three-year-olds do not think in decades as I did when I realized I needed to get a master's degree to get my promotions on time. Decade goals have the added benefit of helping avoid the biological clock blues experienced when some people reach their thirties, forties, or fifties. I'm not sixty yet, but I'll let you know what happens when I get there.

Climbing the Corporate Ladder

$20,000 a Year

Like most economically-challenged kids growing up, I learned
to appreciate the value of a dollar early in life. To earn a little
spending money when I was about thirteen years old, I used to
go with my Dad to help him with his third job as a janitor
between midnight and 4:00 a.m. on Friday nights since there
was no school the next day. Dad would also let me go with him
one night during the week if I completed all of my homework
and my grades were still good. Having a few dollars that were all
mine was a great feeling, especially since I worked for them.

As soon as I turned sixteen, I was able to drive, which
opened up a lot more opportunities for odd jobs to make
money for things Mom and Dad could not afford to buy us.
One such job was working at a neighborhood grocery store after
school and on Saturdays. I can still remember driving home one
day from the store when I consciously thought about my first
dream in life. Having gotten a taste for earning money, I
thought to myself how great it would be to have a good job
making $20,000 a year. I even said it out loud. I had heard that
with $10,000 a year in income you could qualify for the then
prestigious American Express credit card, and I dreamed of
having two of them.

I did not know how or when I would achieve such a goal,
but that became my dream. Plus, I thought $20,000 a year in
income would probably provide a comfortable lifestyle in 1961
dollars, one where I would not have to work three jobs like my
Dad did to live comfortably.

After graduating from Morehouse College in 1967, I started
my first good job with the Department of the Navy in Dahlgren,
Virginia. I had no idea where Dahlgren was located other than
somewhere in Virginia, but my starting salary was $7,729 a year.

My performance was consistently rated outstanding, but
each year my promotion was delayed one month longer than

someone who had started there at the same time I did. When my boss at the Department of the Navy finally told me that my promotion had been delayed each year because I lacked a graduate degree, I decided to earn a master's before I was thirty years old. I was twenty-three when I made that decision, and it was, in a sense, not an easy one to make. College had been hard for me, and upon graduating I made a pledge to myself never to set foot in another classroom again. But, when I thought about it, my dream of making $20,000 a year was clearly far more important than staying out of the classroom forever.

I decided to get a degree in computer science because it was one of the fastest growing professions in business in the 1960s and 1970s. A fast growing profession meant a lot of career opportunities and, presumably, a lot of compensation. I still had this "make a lot of money" idea in my head.

Purdue University was one of the schools to which I applied because I had read somewhere that it was one of the top five (also most difficult) computer science schools in the country. Even though I had found college work difficult, I was determined to attend a top graduate school because I had not only learned that I needed a master's degree, but it needed to be from a school with a well-respected reputation. I did not want to do all that work to get a master's degree and then be told later in my career that the degree was from a weak school or program.

Although I applied to several graduate computer science programs, the one I really wanted to attend was Purdue's. My boss didn't think I would get accepted at Purdue and, *if* I did, he did not think I would be able to complete the program. One of the program's toughest requirements was to maintain a B average throughout all courses (3.0 out of a possible 4.0).

I did get admitted to Purdue, and I always remembered what Mr. C. S. Johnson, my high school math teacher, had told me: *You might have to work a little harder and a little longer to succeed.* At Purdue I had to work a lot harder and a lot longer every night I was there. As a result, I finished the program in twelve months with a 3.4 grade point average and received my master's degree in 1971.

When I returned to my work unit at the Department of the Navy, working for the same boss who did not believe I could complete the requirements, I was promoted to a GS-13 supervisory mathematician with an annual salary of $20,001. I had turned my dream into various en-route goals and accomplished my decade goal (earn $20,000 a year) at age twenty-six instead of thirty. I was now four years ahead of schedule.

Vice President

My father worked most of his career at the Coca-Cola Company in Atlanta. As Dad moved up in the chauffeur's ranks at the company, he was eventually asked to be the full-time chauffeur and personal assistant to the chairman and CEO of the company, R. W. Woodruff. This was a coveted position among Dad's fellow workers, even though it was a 24/7 job most of the time.

My image of a corporate executive came mostly from my dad's experiences, from magazines, and from television. I did not personally know anyone who was CEO, president, or vice president of *anything*, though I imagined that such CEOs made a lot of money and enjoyed both social prestige and a nice lifestyle. One day, this image became my dream and I said it out loud. "I want to be vice president of something for somebody, somewhere, someday." This meant that I had to leave my job with the government, because vice president of the United States was not what I had in mind. I needed to be working for a corporation if I wanted to climb the corporate ladder.

I put together my résumé and, as a courtesy to Dad, I was given an interview with the Coca-Cola Company. Bob Copper, who headed a corporate analysis group in Atlanta, conducted the interview, but he informed me right from the start that no jobs were available. I thanked him for his honesty, and we had a great talk anyway.

About two weeks later, Bob called me and asked if I would return for a visit with his boss and a couple of other people. When I asked why, he said I had exceeded his expectations during our meeting, and he was trying to convince his boss to create a position for me. He succeeded, and I came aboard.

After nearly four years of working at Coca-Cola in Atlanta, I started to suspect that a vice presidency was not in my future there. I enjoyed the company while working on some great projects, but I felt like I was stuck in neutral. I knew I had to make some changes because I observed how Coke's then-current vice presidents had ascended to such prestigious levels in the company.

If I wanted a chance at becoming a vice president at the Coca-Cola Company, I could remain with the company for a long time, get a position in fountain sales or marketing, and *then* work my way up, or I could go to another company. I chose to go to another company if the opportunity came along, because just as there were low expectations of the "chauffeur's son" prior to the interview with Bob Copper, my suspicion was that the same attitude would persist during my climb at Coca-Cola no matter how well I performed.

Sensing limited opportunity at Coca-Cola, I happened to read an article on the front page of the *Wall Street Journal* about Bill Spoor, the chairman and CEO of the Pillsbury Company (TPC). Spoor boldly stated that in five years TPC would grow from $1.5 billion in revenue to $5 billion. This objective seemed extremely aggressive to me, since it had taken TPC 107 years to get to its then-current sales level. Even without knowing how he was going to turn this dream into reality, I could envision the potential opportunities presented, and problems caused, by such a rapid growth rate.

Ironically, Bob Copper, my boss at the Coca-Cola Company, resigned about two weeks after I saw that article and joined

TPC. I thought Bob either had impeccable timing, or he was just one smart dude. A few months later, Bob made me an offer to join his group at Pillsbury. I chose to join Pillsbury to put myself in a better position to get to corporate vice president, since I had already concluded from reading the *Wall Street Journal* article that my chances might be better there than at Coca-Cola.

When I joined Pillsbury, I was thirty-two years old. My next decade goal was to reach vice-president by the time I turned forty. I was not sure if it was going to happen at Pillsbury, but at least I would be in a better position if I were there. I chose forty as my objective because forty-five was a typical age for corporate vice presidents, and I had hoped I would at least be within shouting distance of that lofty perch by the time I was forty. And, if I were not close by that time, I would have to consider changing my deadline. But I *never* considered changing the dream itself.

My hunch about Pillsbury was right. Bob Copper had hired me to help him establish the Corporate Business Analysis function as a well-respected decision support entity within the company. We did just that, and in the process I learned a lot and gained a lot of exposure to many of the senior executives in the company.

About eighteen months later, Bob was promoted to Vice President of Strategic Planning for Pillsbury. At the same time I was promoted to Director of the Management Information Systems (MIS) Department of Pillsbury's largest division. Today MIS is called information technology in most companies.

As head of the MIS department, I was reporting directly to the president of the Consumer Products Division and reporting functionally to the corporate Vice President of Systems, John Haaland. My biggest leadership and technical test came when Pillsbury acquired the Green Giant Company. I was responsible for integrating its MIS department into the Consumer Products Division's MIS Department. There was obviously a lot of redundancy in systems and positions that had to be eliminated without disrupting the services to the businesses. Many executives, including the chairman and CEO, Bill Spoor, were nervous that if we did not execute the integration smoothly, we could shut down the day-to-day operations of the largest and most profitable division of the company. Gulp!

The integration went as smooth as silk. Less than a year later, John Haaland called to let me know that he was resigning to pursue *his* dream and that I had been selected to replace him as corporate Vice President of Systems. It also happened that the Pillsbury World Headquarters Project was behind schedule and over budget, and administrative services needed a home, so John recommended that those functions report to me as well. Bill Spoor agreed, and I was appointed to be the newly titled Vice President of Systems *and Services.*

When Pillsbury appointed me vice president, I was thirty-four years old, which was six years earlier than I had dreamed. My biggest challenges in the job were to get approval from the Pillsbury Board of Directors for a new multi-million-dollar computer facility, get it built, get the new computer installed, and get all the systems running smoothly. We met all those challenges.

Simultaneously, I was responsible for leading the completion of the Pillsbury World Headquarters Project. This was a decision-making, coordination, communications, and logistical nightmare. My previous boss, John Haaland, had told me that the new computer project was well-planned and well-staffed and, because it was moving along smoothly, it would require little of my time. But he also told me that the World Headquarters Project was a mess and would require all of my time and more.

It took about two years to complete the new computer facility and to complete the World Headquarters Project. The World Headquarters Project was completed ahead of schedule *and* below budget. Two years later, I was presented a Symbol of

Excellence in Leadership Award by the Pillsbury Company. Mr. Spoor himself made the presentation.

Things were now running so smoothly that I started to get bored. I needed a new dream.

Vice President Again!

One day while in my office on the thirty-first floor of the Pillsbury World Headquarters building, I started to reflect on what I had enjoyed the most over the previous two years. It was the excitement of making decisions that made things happen.

I also started to imagine the excitement of being in charge of a business instead of being in charge of a project or large functional area. I knew I was not afraid to be in charge, nor was I afraid to take charge when I had to do so. I also thought about my father's failing health and how, starting from nowhere, he had touched so many lives in a positive way. I started to imagine the chauffeur's son as president of something. I said the words out loud, and my new dream was born.

Once again, though, I had to put myself in position to turn that dream into a series of goals. This led to the bumpy Burger King fast track program. It was bumpy because I had to survive resentment from within Burger King, sabotage, and a plot to get me fired by some higher-ups who were threatened by my performance and reputation for results.

The resentment came from the fact that, as a former vice president with the parent company, Pillsbury, I was going to deny a Burger King veteran one of the coveted regional vice president positions. Never mind the fact that Burger King's top management wanted to broaden the experience base of its regional vice presidents or that tenure alone was no guarantee for success.

The sabotage happened when I became a restaurant manager for the first time. One of the assistant managers purposely removed $50 from the store's cash receipts to cause the daily settlement report to be short. When I counted the cash and compared it to the register receipts, the cash was short by exactly $50.

I stayed there all night trying to figure out what was wrong, counting and recounting and recounting, asking myself if I'd done something wrong or if the register tapes were incorrect. It drove me nuts! I didn't leave until the opening manager for the next day arrived. I finally gave up and reported the shortage on my daily report. I closed the following night and guess what happened? Now, the cash was $50 *over*, which I also indicated on my report. During my last week as restaurant manager at this restaurant, the assistant manager who had removed and then replaced the $50 confessed and apologized to me for what he had done. He felt badly about it because he had come to respect me for what I had done to help the restaurant succeed and for my sincerity when dealing with people. I accepted his apology. He also explained that it was common knowledge throughout the Minneapolis region that the vice president of the region wanted me to fail. This was confirmed by several other people who worked in the region as I was leaving to become the Philadelphia region vice president.

The plot to get me fired played out during my tenure as vice president of the Philadelphia region. It involved my Pillsbury background, a direct report, a franchisee, and a higher-level officer of Burger King who felt threatened by my performance. Following a reassignment of region reporting relationships, my new boss, Bill DeLeat, then an executive vice president of Burger King Corporate, came to visit my region to determine firsthand how things were going. The financials were all exceeding our annual targets, but as Bill put it, "There are a lot of people in Miami [corporate headquarters] who do not like you and want you fired."

I felt crushed since after only a year and a half as regional vice president, my region was exceeding its performance goals. After spending about three intensive days in my region, Bill also told me that it was unquestionably one of the best regions, if not *the* best region, in the company.

Bill started a campaign in corporate to correct the unfair and inaccurate perception of my performance. Bill DeLeat was one of those angels for whom you can only be thankful, especially when things are so unfair. Since the corporate attitudes toward me were personal and not performance based, they did not change much, but Bill provided strong support and watched my back while I kept doing my job. If handled differently, the entire episode could have ended my corporate career. Period.

After three years of running the Philadelphia region, I received a phone call from Jeff Campbell while attending a regional vice president's meeting in San Francisco. Jeff had been president of Burger King before being promoted to an executive position at Pillsbury, where he was in charge of all the restaurant companies. Jeff was my boss's boss's boss, and although I knew him and had a good relationship with him, he didn't have time to be calling me out of a meeting just to say hello. I returned Jeff's call and after the usual small talk, he said he wanted me to meet him in Miami to talk about taking over as president of Godfather's Pizza, Inc., another newly acquired restaurant company. I said, "Did you say 'president'?" He said yes. Another flashback!

President

I took over as president of Godfather's on April 1, 1986, at the age of forty! I was now twenty years *ahead of plan*, and I was loaded with "frequent dreamer miles." I headed Godfather's for ten years, which included buying the company from Pillsbury, because it did not believe Godfather's could survive (another likely situation for an unlikely candidate). I was also asked to join several corporate boards of Fortune 500 companies, which was an unexpected experience and benefit of becoming president of "something." When dreams turn to a series of goals, you sometimes find some unexpected "goal dust."

I did not have a new dream in 1996 when I was asked to become president and CEO of the National Restaurant Association. I had already exceeded my wildest imaginations throughout my career. The association job seemed like it would be a challenge for a while, and for the two and a half years I was there, it *was* a challenge. I felt good about our accomplishments.

I had always been goal-oriented ever since I wanted to help Dad with his night janitor's job to make spending money. The concept of decades goals had to be God-inspired to keep me focused, because I realized long ago that God put me on a fast track of success for reasons that are still unfolding. Sometimes those reasons include an unanswered question.

The Question

The series of events and their amazing sequence that led up to my decision to run for the Senate can only be explained as divinely directed.

It started with the birth of my granddaughter, Celena. On January 20, 1999, while attending a National Restaurant Association Board meeting in Maui, Hawaii, I received a call from my wife Gloria. Our daughter Melanie, she said, was about to have her baby, so Gloria would be flying from Omaha to Atlanta that day (a Wednesday) to be with her.

I told Gloria I would finish my meeting in Hawaii and head to Atlanta, too, but that I would probably not arrive before Melanie delivered her baby, since I had an important previously-scheduled get acquainted meeting on Friday in Austin, Texas, with then-governor George W. Bush. I got to Austin on Thursday and stayed overnight, as planned. I continually called Gloria to make sure everything with Melanie was going normally and to find out if I had become a granddad yet.

Melanie's doctor, I learned, had sent her home several times from the hospital, each time because, in his opinion, she was experiencing false labor pains and did not need to check into the hospital yet. Each time Melanie, husband Dobie, and Gloria returned home, Melanie would feel more pains and they would take off to the hospital again. This continued until Friday morning, when the doctor finally admitted Melanie to the hospital. I was still calling in for frequent updates.

After my meeting on Friday afternoon the 22nd, which lasted from 3:00 to 4:00 p.m., I rushed to the Austin airport to catch the first nonstop flight to Atlanta. I arrived in Atlanta at about 9:00 p.m., rented a car, and drove to the hospital, arriving there at 9:30. My son Vincent was in the waiting room, and he told me that the baby had not arrived yet but that everything was still going okay.

At 9:56 p.m., Celena Patrice came into this world. A few minutes later, Gloria came out and told Vincent and me, "We have a granddaughter, and Vincent has a niece." We were excited, but Gloria wore a somewhat exasperated look on her face.

When I asked what was bothering her, she explained, "I have been with this girl for three days, going back and forth to the hospital. I have been in the delivery room with her, dealing constantly with hospital personnel. And then you show up and the baby is born." I told her that Celena was just waiting on Granddad before making her appearance. Gloria said, "I know, and I will have to hear this story for the rest of my life."

A few minutes later, I was allowed into the delivery room. Melanie was doing fine, a small blanket wrapping the new bundle in her arms. I smiled as I looked at Melanie and said, "My baby daughter has a baby daughter." Melanie, a big smile on her face, asked me if I wanted to hold my new granddaughter. Of course I did!

When I took Celena in my arms and looked at that tiny, fifteen-minute-old face, the first thought that ran through my mind was not "How do we give her a better start in life?" as our parents had done for us, and we had done for our children. My first thought was "How do I make this a better world?"

That question resonated in my head and impacted every decision I made from that day on. I did not know the answer, but I could not forget that question. During those moments as I looked at Celena's little face, I thought about all the other little faces around the world and the kind of world we would leave to them. Though we were blessed to live in the greatest country in the world, our greatness was slowly slipping away for a lot of reasons.

In the last fifty years, this nation had made a breakthrough technological achievement by landing on the moon. That achievement started with a strong declaration by President John F. Kennedy that we would land on the moon by the end of the decade of the sixties, and we did so in 1968. The determined leadership of Dr. Martin Luther King Jr. touched the heart of America and the world, which resulted in the historic Civil Rights Act of 1964. President Ronald Reagan's persistence against Communism resulted in the wall crumbling down in 1990. We survived two wars, a nuclear threat by the then Soviet Union, and several terrorist attacks against our country's installations abroad. These and other accomplishments would not have been possible without strong leadership, a strong national resolve, and a strong and resilient economic infrastructure.

Yet, in that same fifty-year period we did nothing to improve the structure of the burdensome tax code, the coming Social Security crisis, and a Medicare system that overpromised and overspent decades ago. We had succeeded at keeping these structures on life support with one band-aid after another, but we were now about to enter at the twenty-first century. More importantly, we were about to leave Celena and all our grandchildren a mess.

For three and a half years I would not be able to answer the question of what do I do to make this a better world. But I would often reflect on the words of the prophet Isaiah (40:31): "They that wait upon the LORD shall renew their strength; they shall mount up with wings as eagles . . . ."

The Answer

In 2000 my wife and I moved back to Atlanta after thirty-five years of successfully "climbing" the corporate ladder. I had sold my equity in Godfather's Pizza, Inc., and had refocused my energies on keynote speaking, writing another book (not this one), serving on several corporate boards of directors, and playing more golf to improve my game. In fact, we even bought a house on a golf course so I would have the convenience of practicing and playing on a regular basis.

Moving back to Atlanta also had the added benefit of living near our adult children and our grandchildren. At the time, both of our mothers were also living in Atlanta and were getting up in age, and we knew that our time had come to help care for them. My father and Gloria's father had both passed decades earlier.

Together, we had achieved a life at fifty-eight years of age consisting of no worries, no drama, and no stress except for the minutia of day-to-day living. To say that we were truly blessed was an understatement. This is what we had worked to attain in all of our thirty-six years of marriage.

But in May 2003 a series of unexpected events started to happen. Steve Moore, a friend and fellow conservative and president of the Club for Growth, called and suggested that I run for retiring Senator Zell Miller's seat since I had come back home to Georgia. I told him I was flattered that he would make that suggestion, but I didn't come back home on the "Midnight Train to Georgia."   Why would I want to run for the U.S. Senate? Why would I want to get involved in the insanity of politics? Coincidentally, several other acquaintances also called and asked me to consider running, so I at least thought about it for a few days. More importantly, I prayed a lot about the idea.

About a week later I called Steve and said thanks for the vote of confidence, but I absolutely did not want to make a run at the Senate seat. My life was in a happy state of cruise control, and I did not want to downshift to start an uphill climb in the elected political arena. He said he understood but hoped I would reconsider.

A few days later I awoke at 4:00 a.m., which was not unusual for me, to read and do some Bible study. I did not have a particular passage or chapter in mind because I had just finished working on a speech that I had been invited to give in May at the Crystal Cathedral's International Men's Conference. As I picked up my Bible on the table next to where I like to read, the Bible slipped out of my hand and fell open on the floor. I picked it up and noticed it was open to the book of Mark and the eighth chapter. Without hesitation, I decided to read that chapter from the beginning. When I got to the thirty-sixth verse, I stopped in my spiritual tracks: "For what shall it profit a man, if he shall gain the whole world, and lose his own soul?"

This was not the first time I had read this verse, but it was the first time it seemed to jump off the page at me. I thought to myself that I had not gained the whole world, but I had gained more than I ever expected to gain. It made me think about giving back more since I had been so blessed. I thought a lot about that verse the rest of the week and about Steve Moore's phone call. I dismissed it as a coincidence.

At church the following Sunday, our pastor, Reverend Cameron M. Alexander, preached a sermon titled "A Calling." He described a calling as *the intersection of your talents and human needs.* When he said that, I felt an incredible rush throughout my body. I knew it was God trying to tell me something.

After the service, I met with Reverend Alexander and shared with him the series of events that had happened over the last several days, concluding with his sermon. I recall him saying, "How much louder does God have to tell you something?" After our meeting I went home and discussed these events with Gloria, and prayed about the idea of running for the Senate some more, and some more, and some more.

I had been extremely blessed with a great life and many talents that I was about to park on a golf cart three times a week. And now four events had said *no* to that scenario—Celena's birth, Steve Moore's call, a dropped Bible, and Reverend Alexander's sermon on "A Calling."

The last week in May 2003, I decided to run for the United States Senate in Georgia.

No Running Shoes

I had never run for elective office before. I was not familiar with the Georgia Republican Party, I had no campaign manager or staff, I had no idea how much money I could or would need to raise, I did not know I was labeled a conservative based on my beliefs, I knew nothing about the political landscape in Georgia, and I had no idea who else would be running. Clearly, there was more I did not know about running for the Senate than what I did know. But I did know that the decision was God-inspired. That's all I needed to know.

I called Steve Moore and told him I had reconsidered and was going to put together an exploratory committee. He was happy to hear that and pledged his help, which he subsequently provided big time, and said he would arrange for me to present to the Club for Growth for consideration of financial support. The Club also came through big time.

My call to Steve Moore happened about a week before I was supposed to give my speech at the Crystal Cathedral's International Men's Conference in California. As I discovered later, my speech at the Men's Conference was on the same weekend as the 2003 Georgia Republican Party statewide convention.

I received a call from someone active in Republican politics who had heard I was running even before I had made the decision to do so. Now that I had decided to run, he suggested I should cancel my commitment at the Crystal Cathedral and attend the state convention. I said absolutely not. I do not break commitments unless I'm severely ill or there's a personal tragedy. More than I could have ever anticipated, that was the right decision.

My next two calls were to Steve Caldiera and Tony Fabrizzio. Steve had worked for me as vice president of communications at the National Restaurant Association when I was president and CEO from 1997 to mid-1999. Tony was a mutual friend and well-known political consultant I met in the early 1990s as chairman of the association. Steve and Tony both asked (in separate phone calls) if I had lost my (expletive!) mind. I met the two of them in Washington, D.C., in mid-June 2003, and when they understood that I had to do this, they offered their help and assisted me in putting together a game plan. The election was only thirteen months away. Thirteen has always been a good number for me because I was born on the thirteenth.

A Dream Invitation

My speech at the Crystal Cathedral was extremely well-received. I spoke on the subject of leadership as discussed in my then-latest book *CEO of Self.* The invitation to speak came as a result of meeting Dr. Robert Schuller through the Horatio Alger Association and through having been his interview guest several times on his weekly *Hour of Power* television program. Dr. Schuller was there for the speech that night, which had a more than normal spiritual tone, since it was in one of the most inspiring spiritual settings I have ever experienced. Until that night, Dr. Schuller did not know that I was also an associate minister at my home church in Atlanta, Antioch Baptist Church North.

About a month later, Dr. Schuller called asking me to give the morning sermon for one of the Crystal Cathedral Sunday services in July while he would be on vacation. The sermon would be broadcast nationwide in August. *Wow!* I thought to myself. It had been an awesome experience just to attend one of Dr. Schuller's Sunday services and then to be his guest for an interview several times over the years. Now I was asked to deliver the morning sermon! I felt humbled, inspired, and challenged. What an honor.

As we talked, Dr. Schuller gave me the date and said he sincerely hoped I could say yes to July 20, 2003. I looked at my calendar, saw that I was available, and immediately accepted his invitation. I was so excited that I did not realize the date was exactly one year prior to the 2004 primary election date for the Senate race I had just decided to enter. Though I had already heard God loud and clear, He was still talking to me.

I was prayerful for about a week as to what I should preach about, and yes, I planned to preach! What message could I deliver to such a vast and broad worldwide audience? Soon the inspiration came. As I prepared that sermon, I knew it was for me as much as it was for others who might hear it.

The sermon was titled "Your Purpose in Life." I delivered it for both services, and it was broadcast around the world in August 2003. The sermon is in the appendix section of this book, and you can hear it on www.hermancain.com.

Little did I know how many people all over Georgia would be watching my sermon that Sunday. It turned out to be thousands and thousands of people, because as I campaigned for the Senate people would constantly remark that they had seen me on the *Hour of Power* from the Crystal Cathedral.

As I said earlier, it was absolutely the right decision, and in retrospect for a whole lot of reasons.

My Journey Continues

My Senate race was another example that "the bend in the road is not the end of the road" in life. My father would probably have added, ". . . if you don't miss the curve." Finishing an impressive second place in the 2004 Republican Senate Primary was just a bend in the road, and I was not about to miss the curve.

Throughout the campaign I felt like I was running at 75 miles per hour, 24 hours a day, and 7 days a week. One of our campaign mottos was, "They will not outwork us." I believe we lived up to that motto. In fact, a field staffperson for one of my opponents asked me one day, "Are there two of you?" I said no, I'm just faster than a speeding bullet.

Election night was exciting and emotional. After all the hard work by everyone on the campaign team, the volunteers, the donors, and sacrifices of so many people, it all came down to this night. Watching the election results come in was one of the biggest thrills of my life. But around 9:30 p.m. my campaign manager concluded that we were not going to force a run-off like we had hoped. It was time to concede.

Although I was disappointed and, by now, extremely exhausted, I was not devastated. We had worked as hard and as fast as we could. We were proud of our second place finish, knowing that many political pundits did not think I had a chance at all. More than twenty years ago, Reverend Alexander preached another sermon that I never forgot. It was titled "When one door closes, another door opens," and its message applies to me today.

When the Senate race was over, I knew I had to slow down and reevaluate, regroup, and refocus. Since that time, new "doors" have opened, and unexpected opportunities are constantly coming my way. Becoming a United States senator would have allowed me to be a catalyst for aggressive change in Congress. That did not happen. Instead, a new foundation, opportunities for radio, television, Internet, and print media have emerged as a new and exciting phase of my life's journey. I do not know where these endeavors will ultimately lead, but I know I know "Who" leads the way.

Stay tuned. I didn't miss the curve!

My Inspired Journey

• I had always been goal oriented ever since I wanted to help Dad with his night janitor's job to make some spending money. The concept of decades goals had to be God-inspired to keep me focused, because I realized long ago that God put me on a fast track of success for reasons that are still unfolding. Sometimes those reasons include the unanswered question: How do I make this a better world?

• I had been extremely blessed with a great life and many talents that I was about to park on a golf cart three times a week. And now four events had said NO to that scenario; Celena's birth, Steve Moore's call, when I dropped my Bible, and Reverend Alexander's sermon on "A Calling."

• The last week in May of 2003 I decided to run for the United States Senate in Georgia.

• My Senate race was another example that "the bend in the road is not the end of the road" in life. My father would probably have added, "If you don't miss the curve." Finishing an impressive second place in the 2004 Republican Senate Primary was just a bend in the road.

• Stay tuned. I didn't miss the curve!

"Your Purpose in Life"

By Reverend Herman Cain

Your purpose in life has two dimensions . . . finding it and living it. Finding your purpose is a process. Living your purpose is a decision. Jesus explained this to His disciples in Mark 8:36: "For what shall it profit a man, if he shall gain the whole world, and lose his own soul?" Jesus had a divine purpose that He had to live out.

We all have purpose in life because God does not make junk. God created all of us on purpose for a purpose, which is revealed to us in phases throughout life, because life is a journey. Moses never expected his journey to take him back to Egypt to become the reluctant leader of the children of Israel. Ronald Reagan probably never envisioned his journey going from radio to TV to movies and then to president of the United States of America. I never imagined being a mathematician, then a corporate executive, and then a pizza company president and CEO. Life is indeed a journey.

Life is a challenging journey filled with complexity and confusion, which can blur our purpose in life and even get us off purpose. The words to the closing song of the 2000 Olympic games reminds us that

> Life can be a challenge.
> Life can seem impossible.
> It's never easy when there's so much on the line.
> But you can make a difference.
> There's a mission just for you.
> Just look inside and you will find
> Just what you *can* do . . .

Our purpose in life is to do what we **can** do, no matter how big or small, using the God-given talents unique to each of us. Some of us were put on this earth to build a great Crystal Cathedral Ministry to provide hope and positive possibilities to millions and millions of people. Some of us were put here to bring a smile to the face of one lonely child.

I'm glad Jesus stayed on His purpose, which was to die for our sins to save the world. After being baptized by John the Baptist, Jesus went into the wilderness for forty days where he was tested by God and tempted by the devil. He withstood the test and did not yield to the temptations by the devil. When he came out of the wilderness he went on a recruiting trip to find the Twelve Disciples. Peter and his brother Andrew and the brothers James and John were among his first recruits. With the Twelve Disciples Jesus went about the land teaching, preaching, and healing. The disciples were constantly amazed as Jesus taught and performed miracle after miracle after miracle among the people.

Then one day, as documented in Mark 8:31-33, Jesus paused with the disciples to do a Bible study class with them. And in this particular Bible study session with His disciples, Jesus informed them of His purpose. He told them that the time will come soon when he will be rejected, he will suffer, he will die an agonizing death, but in three days (the good news) he will rise again. The disciples were disturbed to hear these things. So much so that Peter pulled Jesus aside and, as the Scripture says, "began to rebuke him."

My spiritual imagination and contemporary vernacular tells me that Peter might have said to Jesus, "Look Master, we have a good thing going on here. Your preaching is drawing huge crowds, four and five thousand at a time. And on top of that, you are able to feed them with just a few fish and some biscuits. Your miracles are healing the sick, giving sight to the blind, making people walk again, and I have never seen anybody walk on water until I met you. So why not just stay out of Jerusalem, skip the suffering and dying, and we can keep doing what we're doing."

The Devil was using Peter to tempt Jesus out of fulfilling His purpose. But then Jesus looked at his disciples and Peter and began to rebuke Peter, saying in the 33rd verse, "Get thee behind me, Satan: for thou savourest not the things that be of God, but the things that be of men."

Jesus teaches us that achieving fame and fortune and just enjoying our success is not our ultimate purpose. It's what we do with the fame and fortune and success that matters most in life. And if we acquire no fame and no fortune, and we can barely make it from paycheck to paycheck, it's what we do with the little that we have that matters. As the familiar hymn says, "Only what you do for Christ will last." The rest is just stuff!

The things that be of men can tempt you into thinking that the purpose of life is to achieve a "quiet prosperity" or a life of indulgence and excess, rather than the things that be of God. The Apostle Paul tells us that those things are faith, hope, and charity in 1 Corinthians 13:13. Purpose in life is revealed through faith, inspired with hope, and used to help others (charity). Purpose means doing the things you *can* do to *help* others on their journey.

Dr. Cameron Alexander, pastor of Antioch Baptist Church North in Atlanta, says you find purpose in life at the intersection of *talent* and *human need*. The apostle Paul calls this intersection charity . . . Corinthians (13:13), "And now abideth faith, hope, and charity, these three; but the greatest of these is charity."

Although my father, Luther Cain Jr., left home at the age of eighteen with just his faith in God, his belief in himself, and his belief in *his* American dream, he did what he *could* do. He did not know where his journey would ultimately lead him, but he knew he had to make that first bold step.

Living your purpose in life is uphill, uncertain, but it can be uplifting! When Jesus dragged that old rugged cross to Calvary, it was uphill. Each day of our lives is an uncertainty because tomorrow is not promised, it's a mystery, but we know who unlocks the mystery of tomorrow day by day. And we have the uplifting joy of knowing that Jesus fulfilled His purpose for us.

Four years ago I discovered my new purpose in life. I did not know which path it would take me down on my life journey, but God had made it crystal clear to me what I was supposed to be about for the rest of my life using everything I had achieved, everything I had experienced, everything I had learned, and some things I had not learned yet. The birth of my granddaughter, Celena, made me realize that I had not completed my purpose.

Finding your purpose in life begins with the *things that be of God . . . faith, hope, and charity. Living* your purpose in life will at times be *uphill, uncertain, but uplifting* at the intersection of *your talents* and *human need*. Just look inside the word of God, and you will find just what you *can* do.

The words of Dr. Benjamin E. Mays describe the tragedy of life without purpose when he said, "It must be borne in mind that the tragedy of life does not lie in not reaching your goals, the tragedy lies in not having any goals to reach. It isn't a calamity to die with dreams unfulfilled, but it is a calamity not dream. It is not a disaster to be unable to capture your ideals, but it is a disaster to have no ideals to capture. It is not a disgrace not to reach the stars, but it is a disgrace to have no stars to reach."

Delivered at the Crystal Cathedral
Dr. Robert Schuller, Pastor
Garden Grove, California
July 20, 2003

Bibliography

Americans for Fair Taxation, <www.fairtax.org>.

Bozell, L. Brent. *Weapons of Mass Distortion: The Coming Meltdown of the Liberal Media.* New York: Crown Forum, 2004.

Brown v. Board of Education. 347 U.S. 483 (1954).

Cain, Herman. *CEO of SELF: You're in Charge.* Irving TX: Tapestry Press, 2001.

———. *Leadership Is Common Sense.* Irving TX: Tapestry Press, 1997.

Congressional Budget Office. *Effective Tax Rates Under Law, 2001 to 2014,* <www.cbo.gov>.

CNN.com. 2004 Presidential Election Exit Poll, <www.cnn.com>.

Hallow, Ralph Z. "GOP to Finesse Immigration Issue." *The Washington Times,* 23 August, 2004.

Janis, Irving. *Groupthink: Psychological Studies of Policy Decisions and Fiascoes,* 2nd ed. Boston: Houghton Mifflin, 1982.

Joint Center for Political and Economic Studies. *National Opinion Poll: Politics and the 2004 Elections,* <www.jointcenter.org>.

Media Research Center's Free Market Project, <http://www.mrc.org/>; <http://www.freemarketproject.org/>.

Miller, Zell. *A National Party No More: The Conscience of a Conservative Democrat.* Atlanta: Stroud & Hall, 2003.

Nagourney, Adam. "Baffled in Loss, Democrats Seek Road Forward." *New York Times,* 7 November 2004, 1.

National Center for Education Studies, <http://nces.ed.gov>.

Netanyahu, Benjamin. "Speech before the U.S. Senate." 10 April 2002, <http://www.netanyahu.org/netspeacinse.html>.

Peterson, Rev. Jesse Lee. *SCAM: How the Black Leadership Exploits Black America.* Nashville: WND Books, 2003.

Plessy v. Ferguson. 163 U.S. 537 (1896).

Rath, Tom, and Donald O. Clifton. *How Full Is Your Bucket? Positive Strategies for Work and Life.* New York: Gallup Press, 2004.

Tharpe, Jim. "Senate candidates court black officials." 27 June 2004. *Atlanta Journal-Constitution.*

Watts, J. C., Jr. *What Color Is a Conservative? My Life and My Politics.* New York: HarperCollins, 2002.

Young, Andrew. *An Easy Burden: The Civil Rights Movement and the Transformation of America.* New York: HarperCollins, 1996.

———. "Elections are Iraq's Best Hope." *Atlanta Journal-Constitution.* 28 January, 2005.

Index of Names

Herman Cain

T oo many voters today feel "politically homeless" because their elected officials abandon leadership on the big issues once elected and do not pursue aggressive policy solutions in Washington, D.C. The *politically homeless* includes Democrats, Republicans, Independents, and registered non-voters who are put off by the scare tactics, deception, distortions, and lack of issue leadership and solutions to protecting our economic foundations.

The *New Voters Alliance* is a home to voters across the country who want political parties, political candidates and elected officials to stop using the same decades-old political rhetoric and "spin" tactics against each other and the public.

They want *solutions* and not *excuses.*

With over 290 million people in this country every issue is most important to somebody. But if we do not stop the gradual collapse of our economic infrastructure, the list of other important issues will become irrelevant.

In order for real solutions to rise to the top of the public's mindset and the forefront of congressional action, we must consistently challenge the status quo and elect senators and representatives who share our passion for change.

The *New Voice*

★ ★ ★ ★ ★ ★ ★ ★ ★ ★ ★ ★ ★ ★

But, helping to get candidates elected with views and opinions consistent with one's constituency is no longer enough to impact public policy. ***Effective follow-up between elections*** is also required using advances in technology, due to the plethora of political forces pulling on senators or representatives after they are elected.

Election Day is not the end of voter influence over the legislative process. *It's the beginning*, because too many veteran politicians campaign on hope and enthusiasm, then return to the status quo and doubt when they get re-elected.

Your vocal, interconnected, and persistent involvement in influencing public policy is the key to growing the *New Voters Alliance* **and saving our economic infrastructure. As a motivated** *New Voice,* **there are no limits to your ability to influence Congress and others on the urgency for aggressive policy solutions!**

Herman
CAIN
New Voters Alliance

VISION

*Enact aggressive economic policy solutions

MISSION

Encourage working people to become
informed and active supporters of
aggressive economic policy solutions

STRATEGY

* Recruit active members in all 50 states

* Establish a Vocal, Interconnected, and
Persistent (VIP) network of influence in
each congressional district

* Influence members of Congress to support
aggressive positions on federal economic policy

* Take an active role in supporting conservative
candidates who support our principles

www.NewVotersAlliance.org